How to be a Web Developer

A Complete Beginner's
Guide on What to Know
and Where to Start

Radu Nicoara

Apress®

How To Be a Web Developer: A Complete Beginner's Guide on What to Know and Where to Start

Radu Nicoara
Berlin, Germany

ISBN-13 (pbk): 978-1-4842-9662-2   ISBN-13 (electronic): 978-1-4842-9663-9
https://doi.org/10.1007/978-1-4842-9663-9

Managing Director, Apress Media LLC: Welmoed Spahr
Acquisitions Editor: James Robinson-Prior
Development Editor: James Markham
Coordinating Editor: Gryffin Winkler
Copy Editor: Kezia Endsley

Cover designed by eStudioCalamar

Distributed to the book trade worldwide by Apress Media, LLC, 1 New York Plaza, New York, NY 10004, U.S.A. Phone 1-800-SPRINGER, fax (201) 348-4505, e-mail orders-ny@springer-sbm.com, or visit www.springeronline.com. Apress Media, LLC is a California LLC and the sole member (owner) is Springer Science + Business Media Finance Inc (SSBM Finance Inc). SSBM Finance Inc is a **Delaware** corporation.

For information on translations, please e-mail booktranslations@springernature.com; for reprint, paperback, or audio rights, please e-mail bookpermissions@springernature.com.

Apress titles may be purchased in bulk for academic, corporate, or promotional use. eBook versions and licenses are also available for most titles. For more information, reference our Print and eBook Bulk Sales web page at http://www.apress.com/bulk-sales.

Any source code or other supplementary material referenced by the author in this book is available to readers on GitHub (https://github.com/Apress). For more detailed information, please visit https://www.apress.com/gp/services/source-code.

Paper in this product is recyclable

Table of Contents

About the Author

Radu Nicoara has worked in web development for more than ten years. Being self-taught, he knows how difficult it is to know what to study and what practical knowledge you need to get started. Because of this, he has spent the past five years organizing and teaching programming courses in Berlin, where he lives and works as a senior web engineer.

About the Technical Reviewer

Kenneth Fukizi is a software engineer, architect, and consultant with experience in coding on different platforms internationally. Prior to dedicated software development, he worked as a lecturer for a year and was the head of IT at different organizations. He has domain experience working with technology for companies in a wide variety of sectors. When he's not working, he likes reading up on emerging technologies and strives to be an active member of the software community.

PART I

Getting Started

CHAPTER 1

Introduction

Welcome to your journey into the world of web development! Since you picked up this book, you must have some interest in the domain. That means that you most likely have what it takes to take your first steps in the fascinating world of programming. This chapter starts with an exploration of what web development is, how it works, and how you can be a part of it.

I wrote this book to explain all the things that I wished I knew before I started along the path of changing my career to web development. There were a lot of ups and downs and hiccups along the way, but to this day I enjoy the process and am constantly learning something new. And I sincerely hope you will as well.

The Purpose of the Book

This book is written for absolute beginners in the realm of web development. I plan to teach you about all the essential skills needed for modern-day web development, the way that it is set up in the largest and most established companies. What I want to do in this book is take you from a full beginner and teach you the skills needed to begin your first week as a newly hired web developer. That means showing you the ins and outs of the various skills needed for software developers to be good at their jobs. These skills are, of course, how to code, where to start, and how to think, but also what to do when you are stuck, the way that development teams work, and the various terminologies and technologies used in modern-day web development.

© Radu Nicoara 2023
R. Nicoara, *How to be a Web Developer*, https://doi.org/10.1007/978-1-4842-9663-9_1

The main plan is that you'll learn to build a Customer Relationship Manager (CRM) application using a modern technology stack. This is an application in which you store contact data about your customers, and some data about the contracts that you have with them.

Building this app will enable you to learn about the topics in context, so that you can avoid having to learn abstract concepts, which are difficult to understand without a concrete example. Going into web development myself, I often found the topics confusing and honestly a bit boring, just to have it all cleared up when I started actually implementing them. Therefore, this book takes a bit of a reverse approach, where you'll implement concepts while you learn them.

But of course, feel free to adapt the project to whatever you feel like doing. Hopefully, by the end of the book, you will have a fully working program, and enough knowledge to be able to start some other personal projects that you have, or even start applying for jobs.

Why Would You Want to Code?

Coding is a tool that can be used as is, or it can help you get better results at whatever else you have a passion for. Imagine programming as a life skill. Similar, for example, to knowing a foreign language or knowing how to drive. You can continue doing other things in life, but a lot more doors open along the way when you have the right skillset. Plus, coding has the added benefit of always being able to offer you a well-paying job. Most of the time it is enough to leave your CV privacy set to public in order to start receiving job offers.

The most important part for me is the following: I wrote this book as an overview about what web development is, and as an introduction to the career that I chose. It is a guided tour into what coding is and what it requires. The main purpose of the book, however, is for you to have fun and learn some new things.

I condense three years of computer science courses into a single book, so I do skip a number of steps. Feel free to research them on your own time while reading this book, if they spark your curiosity. What I aim to do by the end of our time together is bring you to a level where you are good enough to start developing web applications on your own.

I started the same way. Just with an overview, and then slowly I got deeper and deeper into various topics. That helped me take my first steps and build my first websites. But one thing I noticed in the beginning was that I had a lot of misconceptions about what a programming job actually entailed. The next section takes a brief look at these misconceptions.

Common Misconceptions

There are a lot of things that people get wrong about programming in general, and they revolve mostly around what a programming career actually means. That is, what you actually do at work.

You must be a whiz at math. In fact, you do not need to be good at math in order to be a good programmer. I myself was pretty terrible at math, especially the more complex parts of mathematics, like calculus. You do not need those things. The only important part is that you can think logically.

Then, despite what many might say, programming is not boring and it does not require you to sit in front of a screen all day. In order to be a *good* programmer, maybe you just need to code. But to be a *great* programmer, you need to build systems that people actually enjoy using and find valuable. That by definition involves a lot of discussions with user focus groups, collaboration, and generally being open and talking to other people. Only this way can you be of great value to your project and your company. If you do not enjoy talking to people, a programming career will still fit you, but the extent of how far it can go, and how productive you can become in it, will unfortunately be limited. You can't hide in the backroom and ignore everyone. You need your team's help, and they need yours.

That being said, of course, you will spend a lot of time with your headphones on, focusing on your task, as well as a lot of time working from home and doing your job. But in order to be great, you need a decent amount of soft skills and a healthy inclination toward human interaction.

On another note, you also do not need to memorize all the commands, and you definitely don't need to know everything by heart. Nobody does. The main characteristic that makes you a developer is being able to split complex tasks into simple structures, which you then put into *if/else* statements and *for* loops. An example of such a logic structure, written in plain English, is: If the user's account is disabled, reject the login process. Or: To each user in the database, send an email.

Imagine programming a piece of code that instructs a car to drive. You have access to a machine that can only understand left, right, accelerate, and break. With those four simple commands, you can take a round-the-world trip. It is the same with when an app. You just need to know the basic commands.

You are too old/young for this. There is no age that makes you any better or any worse at programming. This is not sports. As long as you have some soft skills, and you can learn a bit of coding, you are needed in the market. That is regardless of your age, sex, religion, or anything else. I would argue that programming is one of the most inclusive career paths, because at the end of the day, all that matters is how good your code is, and how much it helps your end users do the things that they want to do.

You need a degree in computer science. There is also a great need for people who have studied other fields. You don't need to get another degree. Programming in itself is only a means to an end. At the end of the day, you will build software that some people will need to perform their jobs and hopefully will also find useful and intuitive. If you have knowledge and experience in the field that you are building software for, you will be almost irreplaceable. I once worked with a young lady who, before switching to IT, worked in Human Resources. Since we were building software exactly for this purpose, she quickly became the go-to person on the project, and the most knowledgeable among us all. So the more diverse your experience is, the more you can help.

The Downsides

Since I have talked about the interesting parts of the job, and the common misconceptions, it's only right to discuss the potential negative sides of a programming career as well.

You will always have to learn. Programming is one of those jobs where it is very easy to get stuck out of the loop. There are always new languages, new frameworks, and new ways of doing things. I would say that every two-three years you will change one of the ways in which you are working. Whether that is the frontend, the backend, the architecture of your app, or where and how you are deploying, programming means always staying on top of the wave. That might get tiring at times and can have the potential to erode your self-confidence.

This also means that you will always find *somebody who is better than you.* This comparison applies to everyone in the field. IT is such a large domain, that there cannot be a single person who knows everything.

You most likely still need some degree. Although it is not absolutely required, web development is one of those jobs where having a degree will open many doors for you. But the up side is, as mentioned, you do not necessarily need to have one in computer science in order to be a top candidate. A degree in any STEM (Science, Technology, Engineering, Mathematics) field is usually just as good, and a degree in a more humanistic domain will still be an advantage. And yes, it is true that you can still be successful even without a degree. But having one will make things significantly easier.

Staying on the topic of hiring, although there is a large amount of open positions in the field, there is also *a lot of competition.* Maybe not as much as in other fields, like music or HR, but you definitely won't be able to simply march into an interview from your first job application. You will still need a bit of patience to find a nice job. This, however, tends to be less of a problem as you progress throughout your career. After having six-seven years of experience, you will find that you don't even need to apply, as you will get unsolicited job offers on a regular basis.

There are no guarantees. Just because you get into a domain like IT, or no matter the specialty that you choose, there is no guarantee that you will automatically earn a good salary, or that you will always find a remote job. It might be significantly easier, but you will still have to fight for it. There is also no certification, no degree, and no credentials that will guarantee a job. You need to be prepared to send about 100 job applications, and go through at least 10 interviews, before you get an offer. If this happens, just know that you are not doing anything wrong. You are simply competing against a large number of people. And the better the job, the bigger the competition. Including the international one.

You will probably need to start small. Whether that is working in a startup, or starting from the first level, you will be a junior for a few years. That might be a bit frustrating, especially if you are switching careers from a domain where you are already relatively established. I discuss this a bit more in the later chapters, but you will most likely not be starting directly into a well-paid job.

I do not want to discourage you in any way by saying this. I just want to set realistic expectations about the current state of affairs in the IT job market. If you manage to get through the rough part, you will find that at the end you will have a fun, well paid career, with good prospects into the future. This book is written to guide you along the way.

Why Listen to Me?

I was first exposed to programming in college, out of a curiosity that I had. I wanted to know how passwords were stored, so that when I come back to a website, they remembered me. I started learning more and more about it on YouTube and created some fun websites. This lead later to an offer to work as a web developer full time. It was the first time that it had crossed my mind that such a job existed. At that job is where I learned all the programming concepts in a more serious manner.

However, the one thing that I lacked was structure. As a result, I ended up learning a lot more things than were necessary in order to do my job. This of course, over time, helped me become a better and more knowledgeable developer. But I wished that I had somebody to show me what was worth learning and what not, so that I could get to where I wanted to go faster.

In the meantime, I have gathered more than 12 years of experience in the domain of web development, and as a result, I decided to write this book. It's a guide about what is worth your while learning, and what you can skip until you get more experience. You might end up loving programming, or you just might not understand what the fuss is all about. All that I want from you is that you give it an honest try. The best thing you can do in life is explore new things.

What Will You Need?

The most important thing that you need in order to start developing is your curiosity. Since you decided to pick up this book, you already have crossed this particular milestone. Along the years, you will keep encountering new technologies, new ways of doing things, and new frameworks. Curiosity about them will keep you motivated to stay up to speed.

There is a saying that development is about slowly failing at your task until it finally works. So besides curiosity, patience to not give up is another important virtue.

Other than that, don't be afraid to try new things. We are all beginners in something, when it comes to life in general, and programming is no different. Every couple of years, technologies tend to change, and better ways of doing things emerge. Therefore, all of us, no matter how senior we are, have to learn new concepts and new languages. What makes things easy is that all of these languages are made by humans, for humans. So if they did a good job on their side, it is pretty easy to get the hang of things.

Other than the right attitude, to follow this book, you need:

- A computer with Internet access. It does not have to be a good computer—an old laptop will do just fine. But the Internet connection is a must.

- Install VSCode. This is a free text editor that you can download from `code.visualstudio.com`.

- Install Node.js from `nodejs.org`. This will be your main way of interacting with the code.

- Install XAMPP from `apachefriends.org`. You need this for the database layer.

That is pretty much it. For most of these installations, just follow the Next ➤ Next pattern, but if you hit any snags, a quick text search on your favorite engine will solve most of your issues.

What Is Web Development?

This section looks at what exactly web development is. It covers the parts of a web application and explains how it is set up and developed. That means how everything works, as well as what you need to do as a developer to get there. In addition to this, this section discusses what a web developer job involves.

What You Will Do at Work

This section starts by covering what exactly a programmer does at work, so that you have a better idea what to expect if you choose to go down this path.

As the name suggests, web development means creating web applications. The most difficult part of this process is the initial setup. I estimate that 60 percent of the hard work goes into a project even before you have your first response on a web page. After that, you have a working example of a feature, which you generally can just copy from. The initial setup is also sometimes called POC (proof of concept), meaning that you get everything to work just enough so that you can have a small demo. From this point, you start setting up your entire web application. Because of this, the initial setup is usually done by people with a bit more experience, since it is a relatively difficult step.

I will, of course, go through setting up everything in the book's project and explain how all the pieces fit together. But in a corporate environment, in the vast majority of the cases, these parts will already be set up. This means that the most common requests that reach your team look like this:

- We need to create a way for our users to leave comments.

- We need additional fields in our online form.

- Just as we save data on page X about our customers, we need a Y page to save data about our suppliers.

- When I click this, I want this other thing to pop up.

- After I save my data, I want to get a notification that lets me know if the operation was successful.

- Write a test that checks if this user has access to this part of the app.

I do not mean to trivialize the type of requests that you will receive, but these examples show you the types of tasks to expect at work. Of course, the more experience you gain, the more you will be included in the business discussions.

The purpose of this book is simply to familiarize you with the various building blocks that will enable you to build what you need.

What Is the Proper Attitude? Impostor Syndrome

Programming is at the same time a relatively easy endeavor and a relatively difficult task. I know this sounds contradictory, but it is true. This means that, on the one hand, you can easily get into programming and start building things on your own, but on the other hand, nobody is an expert at anything.

You will begin a project, figure out that you don't even know where to start with a certain thing, begin searching for solutions, try a couple until it works, and then 15 minutes later, you will have to start Googling all over again.

Even after all of these years, I still would have significant difficulties doing any work without searching for even the most trivial of examples every five minutes.

For that reason, I want to convince you of the following points:

- **Trust yourself.** Just like long distance running, the key is not to give up, but to go at your own pace. As long as you are ambitious enough to go through a page of search results and continue searching, you are more than half the way through to becoming a programmer.

- **Don't compare your speed with other people's.** We all are good at different things, and it is exactly this diversity that makes our teams strong and resilient.

12

Everyone will feel like an impostor sometimes. From beginners working in a startup, to senior engineers working at well established companies, we all sometimes doubt ourselves. Just keep on going and have fun doing it.

How to Find the Things That You Need

Searching for what you need is the most important part of being a programmer. There is no one person who knows everything by heart, for the simple fact that languages and frameworks keep changing and evolving. That is why a good searching ability is an integral part of your day-to-day job. Although most of it involves simply searching around the web, here are some tips on how to do it better:

- If your questions are about a certain programming language, or how to correctly use any type of operation within it, try W3Schools.com. I personally use it relatively often, and I have to say that it is one of the best refreshers or crash courses into any language, be it PHP, HTML, JavaScript, or React. In fact, I advise you to look at this website either way, as it is a great resource for learning.

- If you have general questions about how to implement a feature, how the setup should be done, where to put your files, or how to start your project, try reading the documentation of the language or the framework that you chose. Out of all the technologies that you'll use in this book, React's documentation is pretty much on point, easy to follow, and also easy to understand.

- If you have a specific question or find a specific error, simply Google the error that you receive. Searches like: "Error: cannot cast string to integer" or "How to parse an array in JavaScript" will most likely take you to *Stack Overflow,* probably the world's biggest online programming community. In my day-to-day job, I perform searches like these at least ten times a day.

About once or twice a year I stumble upon an error that I cannot find on Stack Overflow. This leaves me with two options: either I try to fix it myself, or I post a question on Stack Overflow and wait for someone to help me. But bumping into a new error is highly unlikely, especially at the beginning of your career. Feel absolutely free to search away. The best programmers are also the best online searchers.

How Does a Web Application Work?

There is a certain procedure that each web page needs to follow, in order for the data to be transferred from the server to your device and displayed properly. Figure 1-1 shows a small schematic on how a normal web page loads.

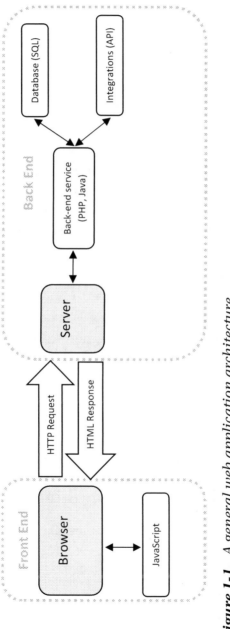

Figure 1-1. *A general web application architecture*

Basically, every time that you want to access a web page, you open your browser and type in the address that you want to visit. This will make your browser access the server registered for that web address and perform a so-called *handshake*. Then the server will take your request, bundle all the data being sent together by your computer (such as the full URL path, form data, your cookies, etc.) and decide based on all of these, what needs to be done with your request.

Once the request is in the hands of the server, it will usually be handled by the so-called *backend*. This is the service that is built in order to interact with the user, usually written in a programming language like PHP, Java, Python, and so on. If it is the case, this service will then access the database to retrieve or store additional data (usernames and passwords) or will try to communicate with other backend services like Google or PayPal using the APIs provided by the vendors.

Once the backend service has finished processing your request, it will pack everything up, usually inside an HTML response, and serve it back to your browser. This includes the data that was requested, as well as the data needed for display, such as styles, images, and scripts, which your browser needs to run on your device in order to interact with you.

These scripts are almost exclusively written in JavaScript, and they contain logic. For example, when a user clicks the Messages button, they open a popup window and ask the server to display the latest messages for this user.

Frontend, Backend, and the Cloud

The *frontend* is the entire bundle of processes that happen in your browser once the data has been provided by the server. The first layer being served is *HTML* (HyperText Markup Language), which contains the unformatted data inside your web page, and additionally all the links to the scripts that are required for proper rendering. Imagine this layer as the data included inside a Word document. It mostly contains paragraphs, headers, lists, and various links to images, scripts, and other pages. An example of HTML website code is the following:

```
<html>
  <head>
    <title>CRM Website</title>
    <link rel="stylesheet" type="text/css" href="style.css" />
  </head>
  <body>
    <h1>My Website Header</h1>
  </body>
</html>
```

Once your system loads the HTML, it will execute the next layer, which is *CSS* (Cascading Style Sheets), and which holds data about how the web page should look. This contains properties such as distances between elements, colors, backgrounds, and so on. For example, the following code affects all elements with the custom_element class, but you will learn more about this in the next chapter.

```
.custom_element {
  background-color: black;
}
```

However, arguably the most important layer is the logic layer itself, which is JavaScript. It was initially built in plain JavaScript, and it was later extended by a library called jQuery, which quickly took over as the preferred way to develop frontend logic. The jQuery library contained a number of prewritten functions such as hiding and showing elements, and sending forms. Now, the most commonly used library is *React*, which was initially developed by the Facebook team, and which you will learn in this book. This framework uses JavaScript to monitor the current state of the page being displayed, and once a certain trigger is activated (such as a new notification, clicking a button, or new data coming from the server), it calculates the easiest way to display the changes, without modifying the entire web page.

The logic layer is responsible for all of the logic inside your page. For example, going behind the scenes to the server and gathering data in such a manner that your page does not need to refresh in order to show the latest data.

The most important part of the JavaScript layer is that it can generate the other two layers (HTML and CSS) dynamically. That means that within the execution of your web page on your browser, different parts of the web page being displayed by your browser will change, appear, or disappear. Having these abilities led to the one-page applications (also known as single-page applications or SPAs) that we currently see all over the Internet. The following code combines HTML and JavaScript:

```
// this button will be hidden once you click it
<input type="button" onclick="this.hidden=true" value="Click
to hide"/>
```

The *backend* is everything that happens within the server. Once your browser reaches out to the server, it will start to compile the data that you want to send back to the browser. This mostly means fetching some HTML and JS (JavaScript) pages and serving them, or providing plain data that it has taken from the database and processed accordingly. This book uses *Node.js* as the backend language, but, as I will discuss later, any other option is just as good. This short code example allows you to connect to the database:

```
// Connect to the database and pull all customers
import DataBaseConnection from "settings";
const connection = new DataBaseConnection();
const customers = await connection.manager.find(Customer);
connection.close();
return customers;
```

Now the question arises: once you finish building your backend, how do you make it available to other people? Where do you deploy it? And what is the cloud? In order to answer that, you need to take a trip 20 years into the past, where if you wanted to host a web page, you would either do it directly on your computer, or if you could afford it, you would buy a dedicated computer (server) and keep it somewhere in your basement. However, with time, it became clear that because of economies of scale, it made a lot more sense to pay somebody a few bucks a month to go through this hassle for you. We now have vendors that group thousands of computers into a single building (called a data center) and sell access to this gigantic network. This is called *the cloud*. It's just basically somebody else's computer.

Classic Websites vs Single Page Applications

Until about 2010, a web application worked in the following way: you would go to the landing page of a website, and your browser would reach the server. The server would then generate a custom web page already filled in with all of your data and provide it to you (see Figure 1-2). If you, for example, clicked a link to see your customer's details, your browser would navigate away into a new page and the process would repeat itself.

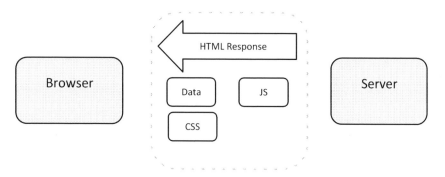

Figure 1-2. *A classic web request*

The disadvantage of this approach is that you always had to navigate away from your web page in order to load data. This could become a problem, for example, if you were already filling in a data form to submit to a different department, but you were just missing just one piece of data. In such an architecture, your best bet was to open a new tab and start searching for what you needed.

Now you can use the *single page application.* You now send an initial browser request to the server, but will receive an empty page. This page contains the basic skeleton of your web application, which will start to get rendered. The major difference is where the data comes from. It is loaded into separate *AJAX* (Asynchronous JavaScript and XML) calls, which load your data one by one. Once the data comes back from the server, the HTML code being rendered by your web page changes dynamically. This, of course, means that you can have pseudo-separate pages of your application working in parallel in the same web browser. Figure 1-3 contains a small schematic of such an application.

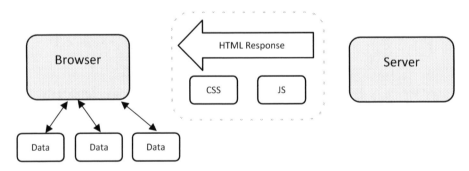

Figure 1-3. *The schematic of a single page application*

The most relevant part of this type of architecture was easy to see when Facebook changed the messaging system. Before, you needed to go to a separate tab in order to access Messenger as a standalone application. But around 2010 they started building Messenger as an integral part of the experience, so that you could read posts and write comments while still having the Messenger open inside the same page. This was all possible because, behind the scenes, your browser can talk to the Facebook servers without the need for you to refresh the page in order to see the latest messages.

The Talk About Programming Languages

You will rarely find people to be more opinionated than developers when they talk about programming languages. This section discusses them as well, to see what all the fuss is about.

First of all, how different are all these languages? Well, not very different at all. The most difficult part of programing is learning your first language, because that is when you learn about data structures, classes, algorithms, loops, and so on. After that point, switching to a new programming language is pretty easy and can reasonably be achieved within a few days.

For the frontend, you do not have a choice in languages, but you do have a choice in frameworks. HTML, CSS, and JavaScript are the only standardized way to interact with all of the possible browsers, so you'll use these languages as they are. However, for CSS one of the most used frameworks is *Bootstrap*, which offers you a set of prebuilt components and styles, like menus, image formatting, alerts, and so on.

For JavaScript, up until a few years ago, *jQuery* was the most commonly used framework, being very well attuned to creating static pages with some internal functionality. However, because of its lacking support for single page applications, its popularity has waned. Most new websites are built in React, a framework used by companies like Facebook, Netflix, Dropbox, and Reddit, to name a few. The advantage of React is that it is a powerful framework that enables you to easily build and reuse big chunks of your code. The downside however is that it is notoriously difficult to learn. Alternatives are Vue.js and Angular, but they all use similar logic. See Figure 1-4.

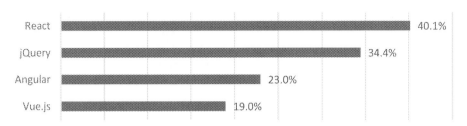

Figure 1-4. *Current use of frontend frameworks [1]*

As you can see in Figure 1-5, the backend is where everything changes. Because the server is completely under control of the developer, the programming languages that you can use are endless. However, the most commonly used languages for the backend are PHP, JavaScript, Java, and Python.

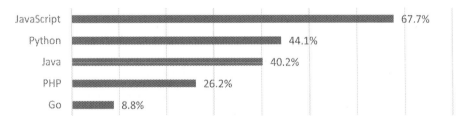

Figure 1-5. *Current backend language use. Some projects contain multiple languages [2]*

The most popular backend language at the moment is JavaScript, and you have to use JavaScript for the frontend either way. Since you already have to know it, why not use it for your backend as well?

That being said, you will use JavaScript for this project of creating a Customer Relationship Management system, both for the frontend and the backend. For the frontend, you will use React, as it is the most popular platform by far, and for backend, you will use Node.js, which is the server-side framework for JavaScript, for the same reason.

Summary

A web application is made up of multiple components. The "frontend" represents everything that runs on the visitor's device. That is the text being displayed, and the way the user interacts with the data being sent back and forth. The "backend" is represented by everything that happens on the server. That is data manipulation and storage, authentication, and processing.

As for the languages, they do not matter that much, but you will stick with JavaScript in this book for the sake of simplicity and of learning languages that are valuable in the market.

PART II

The Tech Stack

CHAPTER 2

SQL Basics

SQL is one of the most important languages when it comes to finding a job. I have had multiple jobs where my day-to-day work involved writing complex SQL scripts. So learning SQL means acquiring one of those skills that takes time to master, but opens a large number of doors.

This chapter teaches you most of what you need to know about SQL. It takes approximately 2-3 hours in total, but it should take you from a full beginner to a mid-user level. I have been in charge of interviewing potential candidates for SQL positions, and I will show you all that you need to know in order to pass the technical tests.

Imagine you are building a new web app. When it comes to storing data on your website long-term, you have to use a database. Imagine the database as an Excel file, where you can use language to interact with the data. SQL stands for *Structured Query Language,* and it is a standardized way of manipulating and interacting with data. There are many types of databases on the market, including MySQL, Oracle, and Microsoft's SQL Server. The difference between all of the offers is minimal in terms of day-to-day use. In this project, you will use MySQL, as it is easy to install and free to use.

SQL is a standard language, so anything that you learn about MySQL will usually apply to any other database that you might use. MySQL enables you to create tables, insert, update, and retrieve data, and delete entries.

© Radu Nicoara 2023
R. Nicoara, *How to be a Web Developer*, https://doi.org/10.1007/978-1-4842-9663-9_2

> **Note**   There are also non-SQL solutions that enable you to store non-structured data. That means that the data being stored does not need to adhere to a predefined structure, but instead it can hold all types of objects, containing all types of fields. However, only 16 percent of applications use this approach, as opposed to the 79 percent that use SQL. This chapter focuses on the majority of use cases.

One powerful resource for this module that I recommend is w3schools.com/sql, where you can find the vast majority of the resources that I talk about here, in a simple and condensed form. I have already mentioned this website, and it is for a good reason. It is an excellent resource for brushing up on your skills in any language.

Installing MySQL

MySQL comes in a bundle called XAMPP. You can download it from apachefriends.org, and then you have to install the package. Once you install it, the command interface will appear, where you need to start the Apache and MySQL services, as shown in Figure 2-1.

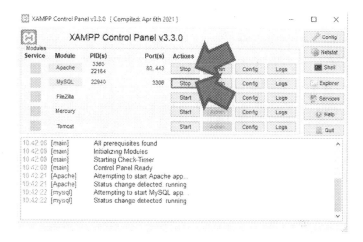

Figure 2-1. *Admin command interface of XAMPP*

Let's look at what you see in the command interface, and what every process that you start up does:

- **Apache** is a web server that enables you to interact with the database using a user interface (UI). It basically compiles HTML and PHP code and provides it to the web browser. If you were to learn PHP, you would do it using the Apache service as well.

- **MySQL** is a service that runs in the background. It listens on port 3306 on your computer (this will matter later), and you can normally interact with it using the command line. But since that is really cumbersome, you will be using the UI in these examples.

Once the services start, access the following URL from your browser: http://localhost/phpmyadmin. This will bring up the UI, and from this moment on, you can start learning SQL (see Figure 2-2).

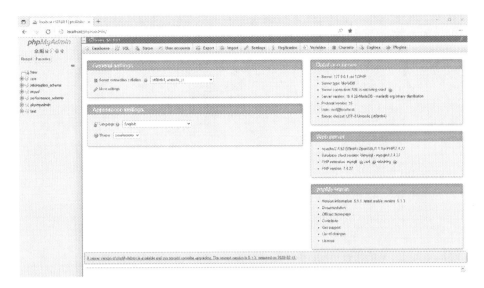

Figure 2-2.   UI of phpMyAdmin tool

Database Structure and Creation

First start with the concept of a database itself. What is a database? In a fundamental way, a database is simply a collection of tables. The reason that people organize tables in databases, and not just lay them around, is the same reason they put files into folders. It brings structure to the entire project, enables hosting multiple apps on a single server, facilitates the split of access, and it also avoids issues with conflicting names.

Now create a new database called CRM. In order to do that, just go to the Database tab, as shown in Figure 2-3, and create a new one.

Figure 2-3. *Location of the Database tab in the phpMyAmin UI*

After saving the database, the system will prompt you to start creating tables. But before you do that, you need to create a logical data scheme for your application. Based on that, you can create the database layer as well, and then build the backend on top of it, and finally, the frontend.

With that in mind, this section starts with a general overview of the types of fields you can choose for a table column. Here are the most commonly-used ones:

- **Integer**. This holds whole numbers like 1,2,3... It is also the default used for the ID that each entity receives, as it can be auto-incremented.

- **Varchar**. A *variable character* is the data type you use for short strings like email addresses, passwords, and names.

- **Text**. You use this for long text data, like comments or paragraphs. The upside of this type is that it can hold a large amount of data, but the downside is that it is difficult to search through, and as a result it should only be used for storage.

- **Date and DateTime**. This is data that you use for events, like creation date, last login, and so on.

- **Boolean**. This holds data of type `true` or `false`, and is mostly used for status checks, such as whether a user was deleted.

Now that you have seen the most used data types, you have to adapt them into your structure. Which begs the question—what kind of data exactly do you want to save into your CRM system? This is exactly the point where building the web application starts—by sketching the database and the relationships.

I suggest that you start by having some customers—the companies that you have contracts with. Then a few contacts will be linked to your customers, to know exactly who to call if you need anything from one of your customers. And finally, a place to store the users who will log into the system, together with their data and their passwords.

This data scheme will look something like Figure 2-4.

Figure 2-4. *Tables in the database*

You will have a list of users that can log in, then a list of customers, and for each customer, a list of contacts. Also, a single contact can be assigned to multiple customers, so this relationship goes both ways. One user will be assigned one customer, but they will have access to see all of the customers. Then you create a list of contacts, and then a page where you can assign a customer to a contact.

Before you start, consider the following standards. These are highly-used in the industry, and will make things clearer for other people using your database. Those are as follows:

- Table names should always be singular. So use customer instead of customers.

- Do not use spaces or dots in names. Either use underscores _ to reference other tables or simply camelCase.

- Every table should have a column that is an ID, auto-incremented, to be used as the unique identifier.

- Every column that links from the current entity into another one should have a name that follows this pattern: TableName_ColumnName

- The length of the column should be as small as you can reasonably expect it to be.

That brings you to the structure defined in Figure 2-5.

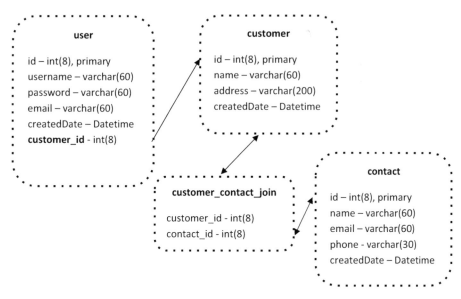

Figure 2-5. *Table structure and content*

Relationships in data structures are of two types: one-to-many (1:M), or many-to-many (M:M). This is also called *cardinality*. In this case, you have a 1:M relationship between customers (1) and users (M), so that means that each user is assigned only one customer, but each customer has multiple users. Therefore, in the user table, you write the ID of the customer that it belongs to by using the customer_id column as a *foreign key* to note the ID of the customer that it is attributed to.

However, a many-to-many relationship cannot be saved into the database directly by using a foreign key, as that can only store one relationship. A many-to-many relationship can only be achieved through a secondary table, also called a *pivot table.* This table only holds the data regarding the relationship between the two tables, which is customer and contact in this example. Note how the tables are named with singular nouns.

Now you can create the tables. Go to http://localhost/phpmyadmin again and open the crm database to create the first table. Your screen should now look similar to what you see in Figure 2-6.

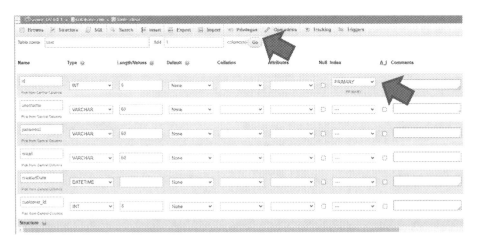

Figure 2-6. *Creating a table in phpMyAdmin*

You need to add the additional columns manually, as initially you only have space for four of them. Or you can add them at a later point, from the Structure tab.

Pay attention to the first column, where you need to select the checkbox for *A_I* through which the column is identified as a primary (unique) key, which also means it will auto increment. This will enable the database to take care of the ID of each entity by auto-generating it and checking that it is unique.

Note that the join table does not have a primary key, as it is defined by the relationship between the two sets of data.

By the end of it, if you click the `crm` name on the left side of the navigation, you should have a database looking like in Figure 2-7.

Figure 2-7. *Result of table creation*

SQL Selects

You will first insert some data into the tables. In order to do that, just select your tables and go to the Insert tab for each of them.

You need to leave the `id` column empty, but feel free to populate the rest of the data. You will see that this will populate the data and generate the SQL code that the app executes in order to insert the data into the tables.

```
INSERT INTO `customer` (`id`, `name`, `address`,
`dateCreated`) VALUES
(NULL, 'Volkswagen', 'Germany', '2022-02-07 21:29:20'),
(NULL, 'Volvo', 'Sweden', '2022-02-07 21:29:20');
```

This is a good time to talk about quotes inside SQL. Note the `` back quotes, which are used for table names and column names, and the '' single straight quotes, which are used to represent string values. There are also sometimes "" double quotes, which are used to assign aliases to tables. You will learn about their functions a bit later.

Now examine the syntax of the previous script. It follows the general syntax of an SQL query. You have an action that needs to be done, then the table where this needs to be executed, and then the additional conditions or values.

Now go to the SQL tab. From there, you can run your queries directly in text format. Try this:

```
SELECT * FROM customer WHERE id=1
```

As you can see in Figure 2-8, the customer with the ID 1 will be retrieved. That is the nice part about SQL. When you read a query, it is relatively easy to understand what is happening.

Figure 2-8. *Result of a SELECT statement*

But this brings us neatly to a question that might have already popped into your mind. Is SQL case-sensitive? The answer is no. The code would work in all caps, or all lowercase, and with or without the back quotes around the table names.

However, the convention is to use CAPS for anything that has to do with the SQL language, and use lowercase for anything that has to do with your data. This just makes thing easier to understand.

In addition, the * (star) part tells the engine to select all columns. For now, it wouldn't make much of a difference if you only selected a limited number of columns, but imagine that you have a table with 200 columns, out of which you extract 10,000 rows. The data transfer would get overwhelming pretty quick.

Therefore, you can select only the columns you're interested in with this command:

```
SELECT id, name FROM customer WHERE id<5
```

As you can see in Figure 2-9, only the columns that you want have been pulled out of the table.

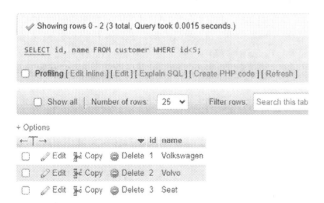

Figure 2-9. *Result of a SELECT with a WHERE clause*

Another skill you need to understand is how search within strings. You can always write an SQL query like this, and it will work without any issues:

```
SELECT id, name FROM customer WHERE name='Seat'
```

This will perform an exact match search, which in some cases might be what you are looking for (such as when you're searching for an email address). However, an issue appears when you want to search for text within the data of a column. For that, you need to use the syntax LIKE instead of the = operator. It provides you with access to the % wildcard, as follows.

```
SELECT id, name FROM customer WHERE name LIKE 'V%'
```

This SELECT only pull out the customers whose names begin with the letter V, as shown in Figure 2-10.

Figure 2-10. *Result of the SELECT with a wildcard*

Similarly, you could write the following query, which searches the customers for an address containing the country, Spain. You do not need to select the column in order to query based on it.

This query

```
SELECT id, name FROM customer WHERE address LIKE '%Spain%'
```

will return all of the customers whose addresses contain the word Spain, at the beginning, the end, or in the middle of the string.

Homework

As homework, try to determine what the following queries will return:

```
SELECT * FROM customer WHERE id BETWEEN 1 AND 10;
SELECT * FROM customer WHERE id = 1 OR id > 10;
SELECT * FROM customer WHERE name LIKE 'BMW%' AND (id = 1 OR
id > 10);
```

Note that when using the AND and OR conditions in the same query, you should use parentheses, in order to avoid unexpected behavior.

SQL Functions

Inside of an SQL query, you can operate different functions, in order to retrieve more complex data. For example, imagine that your boss asks you how many customers you have in the database. The following query will return the number of rows from the table, shown in Figure 2-11.

```
SELECT COUNT(*) FROM customer
```

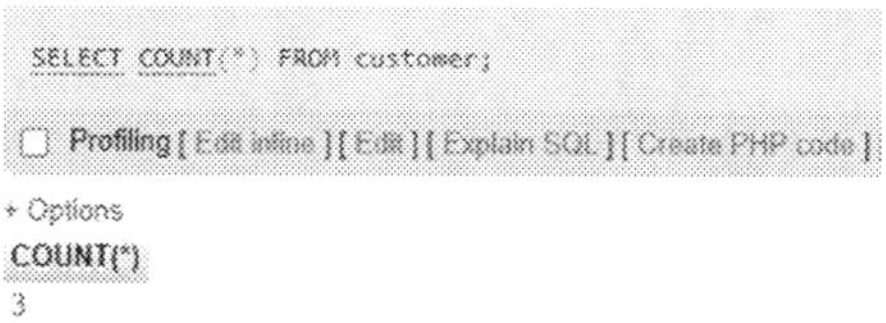

Figure 2-11. *Result of a count function*

As you can see, the name of the column is COUNT(*), which would not help you a lot if you exported this data and give it to your boss. Therefore, you can use an alias for the extracted column (see Figure 2-12):

```
SELECT COUNT(*) AS "Total Customers" FROM customer
```

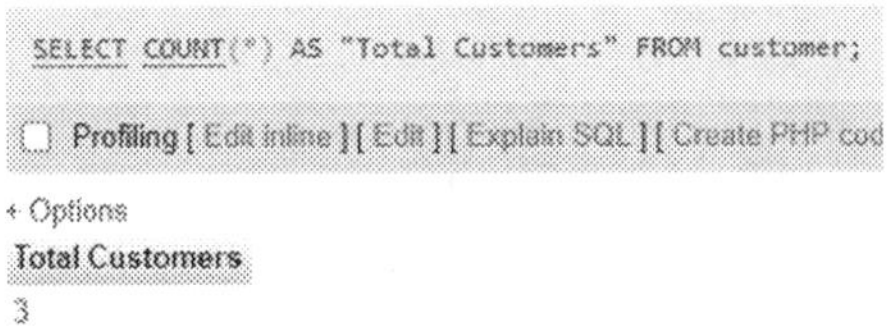

Figure 2-12. *Result of a count with an alias*

This is indeed the place where you must use double quotes. Using an alias simply makes your column easier to understand and a bit more user-friendly. You don't do this only for your users, but also for other developers, if in a few years you (or someone else) have to go back over the code and change something.

You can also use functions that sum up data, calculate an average difference, and so on. For example, suppose you also stored the age of your users inside the database. You could run the following query in order to determine their median age:

```
SELECT AVG(age) AS "Average Age" FROM user
```

Or, if you have a table with contracts, you could run this query to retrieve all of your sales for 2022:

```
SELECT SUM(total_billed) AS "Annual Sales" FROM contracts WHERE
date BETWEEN '01-Jan-2022' AND '31-Dec-2022'
```

As you can see, writing SQL queries is not difficult at all. It takes a bit of getting used to, that is true. But you will quickly be able to pull out data that you need without even thinking twice about the code. That is the beauty of SQL. If you can articulate it, you can put it in code just as easy.

SQL Joins

This might be the most complicated problem of SQL, and the part that most people have issues understanding. Imagine you have the following problem: You have a number of users, and each user is assigned to a certain customer. Holidays are coming, so you ask user to send a letter to the customer to whom they are assigned. This means that you need to pull a list of all the users, together with the addresses of their assigned customers.

In order to do that, you need to do a JOIN operation. This is a way in which you can pull related data from two different tables at the same time. First of all, you need to understand the types of joins, which are illustrated in Figure 2-13.

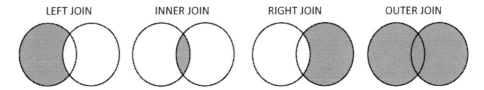

Figure 2-13. Different types of joins

The type of join basically represents the relationship between data that is getting get pulled, and also explains which data should get excluded in the selection. The large majority of joins are LEFT JOINS, so if you ever don't know which one to use, try a LEFT JOIN first.

Now for the syntax. You start with a simple SELECT statement from the base table, and then you join into the second table, by explaining the condition between the two tables. Therefore, the join will look like this:

```
SELECT * FROM
TABLE_1 LEFT JOIN TABLE_2
ON TABLE_2.COLUMN = TABLE_2.ANOTHER_COLUMN
```

Pay attention here. You always have a table on the left side of the JOIN keyword, and always a table on the right side of the keyword. This also means that one column of first table needs to be left of the = operation, and one column of the second table needs to be on the right of the = operation.

That makes the query, based on the database, look like this:

```
SELECT * FROM
user LEFT JOIN customer
ON user.customer_id = customer.id
```

Figure 2-14. *Result of a join operation*

The query will retrieve all the data found in the first table, user, and for each row, any data found in the second table, customer.

The LEFT JOIN operation covers a 1:M relationship, and it does this perfectly. But then this raises the question: What do you do with a M:M relationship? The answer is simple: you perform multiple joins.

Taking a look at Figure 2-14, you can see that the relationship between customers and contacts is held together using a pivot table. This means that you first have to do a JOIN operation from the customer table into the customer_contact_join table, and then from that point on, link the pivot table to contact (see Figure 2-15).

```
SELECT * FROM
customer LEFT JOIN customer_contact_join
ON customer.id = customer_contact_join.customer_id
LEFT JOIN contact
ON customer_contact_join.contact_id = contact.id
```

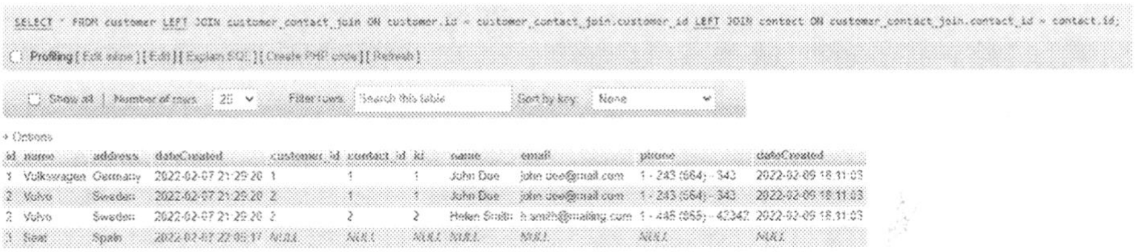

Figure 2-15. *Result of a join operation with pivot table*

That is the way that you link multiple joins together. So, once again, all you have done is one join into the pivot table, and from that point on, another join into the contact table.

This is likely the most complicated question asked in an SQL interview. As long as you have all of your joins mastered, you should do just fine in any technical interview.

Indexes

Say that your business explodes in one year, and now you have over a million customers. That means that you need to consider the performance of the entire database.

Imagine that you are running the following query:

```
SELECT * FROM customer WHERE id = 3
```

And imagine the data looking like this inside of the stored table:

ID	Name	Address
1	BMW	Germany
2	Volvo	Sweden
3	Tesla	USA
4	Seat	Spain
...	...	...

In order to execute the query, the database engine has to open the file where the data is stored and start looking for the ID column where it is equal to the value provided. However, since the primary key of the table is the ID column, the data is already ordered by ID, so the search will be incredibly fast.

But now imagine that you need to run the following query:

```
SELECT * FROM customer WHERE name = "Seat"
```

The database will now have to go through the table one row at a time, and see if the name matches what you need. You can imagine that if you have one million rows, this would take a while.

Therefore, if you could have a copy of all the rows, stored directly and sorted alphabetically by name, this could help. That is called an *index*.

```
CREATE INDEX customer_name_index ON customer (name)
```

This will create a hidden table that will look like this:

Name (Sorted)	ID
BMW	1
Seat	4
Tesla	3
Volvo	2
...	...

It will only be a mapping of the column being sorted, and the primary key.

Indexes are the fastest way to improve the performance of any system. Consider the following advantages and disadvantages of adding a new index:

Advantages	Disadvantages
• Fast and easy way to improve reading speed • Easy to modify and delete if it's no longer needed	• Increases the speed of writing, as every row needs to be inserted into every index • Increases the space required on the machine by a tiny bit

Homework (5-15 Mins)

In order to better understand SQL, try to write queries for the following requests:

1. Select all users whose email ends with .com *(Easy)*.

2. Select all customers who are assigned to a user whose email ends with .com *(Medium)*.

3. Select all the contacts of the customer that
    are assigned to a user whose email ends with
    .com *(Hard)*.

Summary

SQL is one of the fundamental parts of any web application. It allows
you to save and retrieve almost any type of data that you might need for
your particular cases. It also allows you to parse through the complex
connections that data possesses, by using JOIN statements.

Since it is one of the primary building blocks of the entire web, there
are multiple jobs that almost exclusively require SQL, such as business
analyst. Learning this skill alone will put you at an advantage in the
job market.

CHAPTER 3

HTML and CSS

A lot of people do not consider HTML and CSS to be programming languages. But whether they are or not, HTML is the way that websites on the Internet send mostly text information to the web users and CSS is the way that you make that text look pretty. They are at the core of web technology, and a good grasp of them is essential to understanding how the web works. This chapter takes a quick look at both technologies.

HTML

HTML is historically the way that the Internet was built. It is not technically a programming language, but a way to store and transfer structured data. This is because it cannot manipulate anything, and it is not dynamic. Regardless of that, *HTML* (HyperText Markup Language) is the building block of the Internet. The structure of HTML is relatively easy to understand, as it involves two things: tags and attributes.

The language is made up of tags containing other tags. This is what gives HTML its structure. Consider this code for example:

```
<exampleTag sampleAttribute="my_text"></exampleTag>
```

Here, you can see an opening tag called `exampleTag` that has an attribute called `sampleAttribute`, and then a closing tag for `exampleTag`. The `</exampleTag>` part at the end is called an "end exampleTag" because of the slash at the beginning, and then the name of the tag.

© Radu Nicoara 2023
R. Nicoara, *How to be a Web Developer*, https://doi.org/10.1007/978-1-4842-9663-9_3

Let's create a simple web page. Open your VSCode application (or any other code editor of your choosing) and create a file called index.html. In that file, create this small website:

```
<html>
  <head>
    <title>CRM Website</title>
  </head>
  <body>
    <h1>CRM Website</h1>
    <p> Welcome to our website. You can go
      <a href="www.mywebsite.com">here</a> in order to
      see our big
      <b>PROMOTION!</b>
    </p>
  </body>
</html>
```

The code that you just wrote will generate a web page like the one in Figure 3-1.

Figure 3-1. *A render of your first website*

Once the file is ready, you can go inside of VSCode to the upper menu, select Run, and then select a browser. Or you can simply go inside of your Windows Explorer and double-click the file. This will open the code and render it.

Now I'll deconstruct a bit what you are seeing here. First of all, an HTML page will always have the <html> tag as a parent, in which you will always find the <head> and <body> tags. These tags are mandatory, so they will always need to be present. If you for some reason omit them, the browser will generate them when executing the code. In the head of the page, you will find tags like <title>, which contains meta-information about the website, as well as links to CSS and JavaScript code. The main role of the head tag is to provide data used by the browser, or various scripts that read the page, like the crawlers that Google uses.

The <body> tag is where the majority of data is stored. Here is where you find header tags such as <h1>, <h2>,... <h6>, paragraph tags (<p>) and links, also known as anchors (<a>), and links that store a hyper-reference attribute (href). You will also find tags used for text formatting, such as <b> for bold, <i> for italic, <u> for underline, and so on.

There are many, many tags that can be interpreted by your browser, and you can find a more comprehensive list at w3schools.com/html. This section goes through a few examples of the most commonly used tags and explains what they mean.

An image can be built like this:

```
<img src="logo.jpg" alt="Logo of our CRM" />
```

Notice the / (end tag) at the end of the tag. This means that the tag is self-contained, as some of them are. This is equivalent to writing:

```
<img src="logo.jpg" alt="Logo of our CRM"></img>
```

Your browser will understand it just fine if you forget the ending tag and leave it open.

Since HTML is supposed to be the way that your computer talks to the Internet, the syntax is not as strict as in some other languages. That way, your browser can render most anything that it comes in contact with.

A list of items can be built in HTML using the following tags:

```
<p>Why our services are good?</p>
<ol>
    <li>We have everything</li>
    <li>We are good for business</li>
</ol>
```

Why our services are good?

1. We have everything
2. We are good for business

You can create an ordered list <ol> or an unordered list <ul>, and both will contain list items under the <li> tag.

One of the most commonly used HTML tags is the <div> element. It simply represents a division inside the HTML block and does not render anything special, other than a new line. But combining it with CSS and JS makes this one of the most powerful tags:

```
<div class="custom_class second_class" id="my_id">
     This is my div
</div>
```

There are two highly important attributes in web that are widely used and that can be attached to any tag. The *class* is used in styling, and inside of this attribute you can provide multiple classes, delimited by a space. The *id* attribute is an identifier that needs to be unique inside of the web page.

As you can see, HTML is not a very complicated part of web development, and you can be learn the basics in a few hours. As you advance in your career, you might find yourself needing different tags, so don't be afraid to research things on your own.

CSS

Cascading Style Sheets (CSS) make up the web layer that offers, as the name suggests, the option to provide styles to your web page. This code generally looks like this:

```
.class {
  background-color: red;
}
```

The language follows a pattern that can be described like this: it begins by defining what exactly should be affected. If it starts with a dot ., it means it will affect the class. If it starts with a hashtag #, it will be related to the ID, and if there is no character in front of the description, it is related to the HTML tag:

```
.custom      ⇒      <p class="custom">Why things are good?</p>
.id_me       ⇒      <p id="some_id ">My paragraph here</p>
div          ⇒      <div>A div element</div>
```

In the CSS language, you start by opening the curly brackets. You then list a property that you want to change, then a colon, and then the new value that you want to give it to it. Then you end each row with a semicolon (;).

All of this should be surrounded by a `<style></style>` element tag within the `<head>` part of the web page:

```
<html>
  <head>
    <style>
      html {
        background-color: #ffaaaa;
        color: #ffffff;
      }
      .header {
        font-size: 18px;
      }
      #some_id {
        color: #00ff00;
      }
```

```
    </style>
    <title>CRM Website</title>
  </head>
  <body>
    <h1 class="header">CRM Website</h1>
    <div class="custom_class" id="some_id">
      This is my div
    </div>
    <p class="class">Why we are good?</p>
  </body>
</html>
```

This code produces the website in Figure 3-2.

Figure 3-2. *A render of your first website, together with CSS*

As you can see, you start by applying styles to the <html> tag. Doing this will apply a background to the entire web page, seeing how the <html> tag is the parent tag of the whole content.

In this case, you only played around with the colors of the web page, but the most important part of using CSS is the layout. This will enable you to place different elements, one into the other, and arrange the structure of the page.

You will now see how to add colors to the elements, just so you can understand this process. For your actual website, you will choose better looking colors.

```
<html>
  <head>
    <style>
      .parent_class {
        background-color: #ccffcc;
        text-align: center;
        padding: 30px;
      }
      .child_class {
        background-color: #ffffff;
        text-align: center;
        padding: 10px;
        font-size: large;
        font-weight: bold;
      }
    </style>
    <title>CRM Website</title>
  </head>
  <body>
    <div class="parent_class">
      <div class="child_class">This is the child class</div>
    </div>
  </body>
</html>
```

As you can see in Figure 3-3, there is a white border around the green div. This happens because the `<html>` tag has a padding applied to it by default.

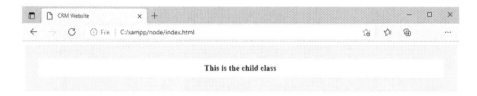

Figure 3-3. *The new website being rendered*

If you want to get rid of that border, you need to add the following code to your style:

```
html {
  padding: 0;
}
```

Note   The `text-align: center;` property was added to the parent `div`, and that means that the child `div` inherited this property as well. This is why the language is called *cascading style sheets*. Because properties cascade from parents into their child elements.

Bootstrap

Judging from what you just learned about CSS, if you start to build a few websites, you will easily see how, every time you start working on a new one, you have to create the same elements over and over again. These elements are, for example, navigation bars, alerts, styled buttons, layout elements, and so on. This is why Twitter decided to build a framework that offers prebuilt website elements, a framework that has quickly become one of the building blocks of the entire web ecosystem.

That framework is called *Bootstrap*, and it is one of the most commonly used CSS frameworks. It basically provides you with a list of preformatted classes that you can add to your elements.

In order to start using Bootstrap, you need to go to the website, getbootstrap.com, and see the offer of elements that they have listed there.

The documentation states that in order to get started, you just need to add two links to the <head> tag and you will be all set. Sounds simple enough, so try it:

```
<html lang="en">
  <head>
    <!-- Required meta tags for mobile -->
    <meta charset="utf-8" />
    <meta name="viewport" content="width=device-width, initial-
    scale=1" />
    <!-- Bootstrap CSS -->
    <link
      href="https://cdn.jsdelivr.net/npm/bootstrap@5.1.3/dist/
      css/bootstrap.min.css"
      rel="stylesheet"
      integrity="sha384-1BmE4kWBq78iYhFldvKuhfTAU6auU8tT94WrHft
      jDbrCEXSU1oBoqyl2QvZ6jIW3"
      crossorigin="anonymous"
    />
```

```
<script
  src="https://cdn.jsdelivr.net/npm/bootstrap@5.1.3/dist/
  js/bootstrap.bundle.min.js"
  integrity="sha384-ka7SkOGln4gmtz2MlQnikT1wXgYsOg+OMhuP+
  IlRH9sENBOOLRn5q+8nbTov4+1p"
  crossorigin="anonymous"
></script>
</head>
<body>
  <!-- Our code starts here -->
  <h1>Hello, world!</h1>
</body>
</html>
```

The meta tags are used here to provide mobile support and proper international characters and help for mobile devices, and the script element is just a JavaScript library that makes the framework function, as you can see in Figure 3-4.

Figure 3-4. *A Bootstrap website*

Okay, this is not very impressive, so you can start to add bootstrap elements into your web page. It is simply a matter of copying/pasting elements from the documentation into your website. Figure 3-5 shows an example from the documentation that they provide.

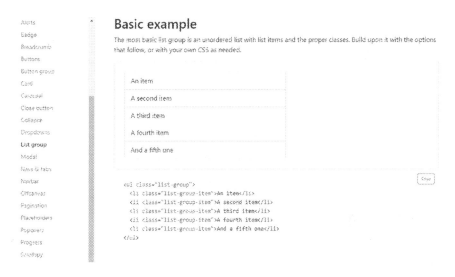

Figure 3-5. *The Bootstrap documentation on getbootstrap.com*

If you simply copy the code into your website, you get Figure 3-6.

Figure 3-6. *The Bootstrap website, with a list group*

I want to talk a bit about layouts. Bootstrap will enable you to split your website into 12 equal columns. Out of these, you can choose if your `<div>` element will take up the width of one column, multiple columns, or all 12, so that the width will cover the entire row. You can just choose the width by providing the appropriate class. Figure 3-7 illustrates this.

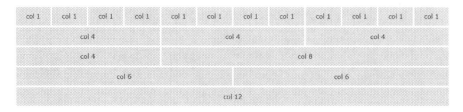

Figure 3-7. *The 12-column system built into Bootstrap, from getbootstrap.com*

If you want to add three distinct columns, for example, you just have to add this text:

```
<div class="container">
  <div class="row">
    <div class="col">1 of 3</div>
    <div class="col">2 of 3</div>
    <div class="col">3 of 3</div>
  </div>
</div>
```

This will render the elements centered and without a border:

1 of 3   2 of 3   3 of 3

Using Bootstrap, the process of creating a website transforms from being this painstaking work of having to build everything from scratch, into the simple activity that I compare to shopping, where you go through Bootstrap's documentation and pick the elements that you need.

I would not even consider building a website from scratch at the moment. The amount of work that before took me three days of setting up, in terms of layouts and formatting elements, I can now do in three minutes of copying/pasting code from the Bootstrap documentation. There is a large selection of websites that will provide free templates of websites already built in Bootstrap, like startbootstrap.com. That means that your website can be 70 percent done when you begin, and your job as a developer will be to adjust things. Work smart, not hard!

Homework

Create your own website using Bootstrap:

1. Go to w3schools.com/bootstrap/bootstrap_ templates.asp and choose a basic template for your website.

2. Go to getbootstrap.com and choose different components to add to your website.

3. Have fun and get creative!

Summary

HTML and CSS are the building blocks of any website. If you only need a static website, adding Bootstrap to it might be the fastest way to achieve what you need. The chapter only briefly touched on all of the possibilities that using HTML and CSS bring with them, and there are entire books covering these subjects. Trying things on your own will provide you with a lot more insight. So this is what I encourage you to do. Try to create a static website and just have fun.

CHAPTER 4

GraphQL and JavaScript

Before you move on to building your app, you need to learn a bit more about the technologies at the core of most modern web applications. This chapter covers JavaScript, the programming language that you will use in your project, as well as GraphQL, which is the modern way to transfer data through an Application Programming Interface (*API*).

GraphQL

GraphQL is a way in which you can communicate with the server side of an application, in order to send and receive data. It is currently one of the newest and most commonly used technologies for interfacing with data between applications, and it is fundamentally the way that your frontend, be it a browser or a mobile app, will communicate with the server side.

Before you start learning about GraphQL, this section explains how things were done before this new technology came along, when most APIs used the RESTful protocol for data transfer. This worked in the following manner.

© Radu Nicoara 2023
R. Nicoara, *How to be a Web Developer*, https://doi.org/10.1007/978-1-4842-9663-9_4

When you'd call for a certain URL, the server would provide you with an encoded block of data in JSON format, as shown here. The content and format of this data was decided by the server backend alone:

`http://my-website.com/mydata/clients`

```
{
   totalReturned: 2;
   clients: [
      { name: "Client1", id: 1 },
      { name: "Client2", address: "Park Lane 71" },
   ];
}
```

This data response was then parsed inside different programming languages like JavaScript without any issues. If, for example, you needed a list of contacts, you would access a different URL, such as `https://my-website.com/mydata/contacts`.

This worked well in most situations, but this approach led to two problems. The first problem was that you did not know what type of data would be returned before you made the call, and that meant you did not know the structure of the data that came back, or what to do with it.

Another issue was that you might not need a big chunk of the data in the first place, and transferring it around led to unnecessary overload. Imagine it just like the SELECT statement inside of SQL. Moving that data around, without it being needed, will first of all needlessly load the server, and will also make the application work significantly slower for the users, by increasing the load time.

Imagine if you just needed a list of all the names of your customers, that you then will display to your users, but in order to access that list of names, you needed to pull 200 other columns that are of no interest, such as addresses, contracts, and financial statements. This is exactly the type of issue that the SELECT statement inside SQL also fixes.

As a result of these needs, GraphQL was created, in order to provide more flexibility in terms of data interfacing between applications. GraphQL helps by knowing the structure of the data that comes as a response and the relationship between different objects being retrieved. It also enables you to retrieve only the parts of the data you need.

So how does this technology work? GraphQL is basically formed out of *queries*, which retrieve data from the server, and *mutations*, which send data to the server.

Say you need a list of your customers, from which you are only interested in the IDs, names, and addresses.

In order to create such a query, you first need to provide the server with a JSON object representing what you want to retrieve from the server:

```
{
    clients {
        id
        name
        address
    }
}
```

The server will return the data that you requested, but only the fields that you specified:

```
{
    "data": {
        "clients": [
            {
                "id": "1",
                "name": "Company1",
                "address": null
            },
```

```
    {
        "id": "2",
        "name": "Company2",
        "address": "Park Lane 71"
    },
  ]
  }
}
```

You can also provide variables to queries that you send separately, such as:

```
query HeroComparison($pageLength: Int) {
    clients {
        id
        name
        address
    }
}
{variables:{pageLength:10}}
```

Mutations, on the other hand, are the way that you send data to the server. In order to, for example, create a new client in your database. They are basically functions that you call on the server side. They may or may not return useful data, depending on what you need them to do, but they will throw an error if any issues pop up during execution.

```
mutation {
    createClient(name:"Big Client", address:"Hall Alley, 54")
}
```

Mutations can, of course, run with variables, just as queries can:

```
mutation CreateClient($name:String, $address:String) {
    createClient(name:$name, address:$address)
}
{variables:{ name:"Big Client", address:"Hall Alley, 54"}}
```

When it comes to building your application, these examples perfectly illustrate the way that you will structure the data transfer. You will create a GraphQL endpoint and have the frontend call it using the queries and mutations, in order to modify or list data.

JavaScript

This section looks a bit at the most commonly used programming language in web development: JavaScript. It includes a short introduction to the language as it is, and helps you get familiar with the quirks and specific parts of JavaScript.

So what is JavaScript, and how is it different from all the other languages?

JavaScript is a scripting language (meaning that the code is not precompiled) that's derived from the Java programming language, hence the name. It was built to be a short, easy way to make a browser do more intelligent things than just display text. It has slowly evolved into one of the backbones of the modern Internet.

The only downside of JavaScript, and I would also say the major disadvantage, is that it takes some practice to get accustomed to the way it is used. It is pretty different from all of the other major scripting languages, like PHP and Python.

Since you have to use it in the frontend either way, because it is the only language that browsers understand, you might as well use it on the backend of your application as well.

Functional Programming

JavaScript is executed "as it comes," so to say. That means that it is interpreted line by line and executed. However, JavaScript also relies heavily on functions. It does this to such an extent that most functions will rely on accepting another function as a parameter, within the broad usage of the language. You can see this in this example showing what a function looks like in JavaScript:

```
function addNumbers(a,b){
    return a + b
}
```

This function will take two numbers as parameters and return their sum. It is one of the most basic functions in JavaScript.

```
console.log(addNumbers(2,3)) //prints 5
```

In order to test this code, open any browser and press F12 (or right-click and choose Inspect) to open the developer tools. Go to the Console tab and add this JavaScript code. The console will then output anything that you set in the `console.log()` function parameters, as you can see in Figure 4-1.

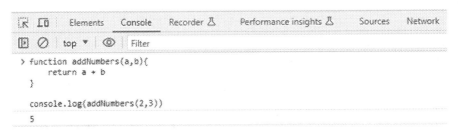

Figure 4-1. *Running the code in a browser*

You can also write a function that takes another function as a parameter:

```
function doubleFunctionResult(originalFunction, num1, num2) {
    return 2 * originalFunction(num1, num2)
}

console.log(doubleFunctionResult(addNumbers, 2, 3))//prints 10
```

This way, in JavaScript, you can use a function in relation to another function.

Constants and Variables

In JavaScript, you declare values as constants, if you are certain you will no longer change their value, or in other words, if they cannot get reassigned:

```
const num1 = 10
num1 = 15 //not allowed
```

If, however, you need to reassign a value, you need to use variables by either using the let keyword or var, which is not recommended:

```
let num1 = 10 //preferred way
num1 = 15
var num2 = 20 //to be avoided
num2 = 17
```

The main difference between var and let is that a let element will only hold its name and value within the block of code that it is assigned to, whereas a var element can "leak" through the rest of the code, possibly leading to unpredictable behavior. As a result, you should always use the let keyword to declare a variable.

A const is better than a variable because it will use less memory. It will also ensure that you don't overwrite something that you don't want to. So you should also try to use const whenever it makes sense.

Functions

There are two distinct ways to declare a function in JavaScript, each with its own variations. They both do essentially the same thing. Consider the first example again, which you saw earlier:

```
function addNumbers(num1, num2) {
  return num1 + num2;
}
```

This is the classic way of declaring a function, but there is a faster way:

```
const addNumbers = (num1, num2) => {
  return num1 + num2;
};
```

This way of writing functions is an even shorter version, but it only applies when the returned value is relatively simple. Here, you can omit the curly brackets and the return statement and directly write what you want the function to return. This is called an *implicit return*.

```
const addNumbers = (num1, num2) => num1 + num2;
//implicit return
```

All of these ways of writing functions basically do the same thing, but declaring a function as a constant is currently the preferred way, mostly for consistency.

Shorthand if Statements

You can write an if statement in JavaScript, just as you can do in any other language.

```
if (message.includes("error")) {
    return " There is an error"
} else {
    return "ALL OK"
}
```

However, there is a easier way to write this, called shorthand:

```
message.includes("error") ? "There is an error" : "ALL OK"
```

               "if" part   "else" part

Using this alternative way of writing if/else statements will clean up your code in most circumstances. Once you start coding, this shorthand will come in very handy, as you will see in the following chapters.

Arrays

JavaScript goes through collections (arrays) of various data structures. Or better said, it parses them. This is because most of the data that will come from the database layer will be in the form of arrays (also known as lists). Imagine you have a collection of customers:

```
const customerArray = [
  {
    id: 1,
    name: "Factory Sky",
  },
  {
    id: 2,
    name: "Gel Producer",
  },
```

```
  {
    id: 3,
    name: "Distribution",
  },
];
```

You can now access each customer by referencing the index within the array, starting with 0. Arrays always start from the index 0:

```
console.log(customerArray[0]) // { id: 1, name: "Factory Sky"}
```

However, imagine that you need an array of all the customer names alone. You can write a function in the "normal" way to do that. It would be the same block in JavaScript, Java, Python, PHP, or any other language:

```
for (let i = 0; i < customerArray.length; i++) {
  return customer[i].name;
} //returns ["Factory Sky", "Gel Producer", "Distribution"]
```

In order to parse the array, you declare another variable to be used as a cursor. Then, you keep adding +1 to i, which is where the i++ the comes from. You keep adding until you reach the full length of the array.

Alternatively, you can use the short map function, which moves the entire code to a single line:

```
const names = customerArray.map((customer) => customer.name)
// returns ["Factory Sky", "Gel Producer", "Distribution"]
```

An even shorter version enables you to rename the variable from the function:

```
const names = customerArray.map((c) => c.name)
```

Map is a function that will take another function as a parameter and run that function for each one of its elements. It always needs to return something. Note that this example used an implicit return statement in the function passed as a parameter to the map function. If, however, you just want to loop though some data and execute code, but not return anything, you will use the forEach function in exactly the same way:

```
customerArray.forEach((customer) => {
  console.log(customer.name + " - " + customer.id);
});
```

This is equivalent to the for loop that you built previously. The forEach function does not necessarily need to return anything, as it will loop though each customer and execute the function provided as a parameter, which in this case just logs the name and ID. But this also means that no new array is generated and returned, so you cannot assign the outcome of the forEach function to anything.

Destructuring and Spread

Destructuring is a procedure in JavaScript whereby you take an object with multiple attributes and push those into separate variables.

```
const customer = { // we create an object first
  name: "Customer1",
  address: "Parkway Avenue 71",
  id: 1,
};

const { name, address } = customer; // we create new variables
out of the object
```

This is the same thing as declaring them separately, but is faster to write.

```
const name = customer.name;
const address = customer.address;
```

Note   The variables must have the same name as the attributes within the object that you are destructuring.

Destructuring works in exactly the same way for arrays as for objects. You just replace the parentheses with square brackets.

The *spread operator* can be seen as the sibling operator of the destructuring process. The spread operator spreads the properties of an object. If you create a new customer like this:

```
const customer = {
  name: "Customer1",
  address: "Parkway Avenue 71",
  id: 1,
};

const newCustomer = {
  ...customer,
  id:2,
  balance:100
}
```

This will make your new customer look like the following code. You can see that the spread operator enables you to add new properties and reassign existing ones.

```
newCustomer : {
  name: "Customer1", //previous properties will be transferred
  address: "Parkway Avenue 71",
  id: 2, //new values will also be here
  balance:100 //new properties
};
```

Promises

A *promise* in JavaScript is a way to tell the code to execute a piece of code asynchronously. That means that the execution will not stop and wait for the code to finish, but will continue to run other things in parallel. You then need to tell the script what to do, once the promise has been completed or has errored out.

Imagine, for example, that you have a piece of code with a function that needs to retrieve some customer data from the server: getCustomerData(). Suppose that this call takes four seconds.

If you write a piece of synchronous code, the execution will stop until the data is returned:

```
const customers = getCustomerData() // takes 4 seconds
allowUserToSeePhotos() // This will not execute for 4 seconds,
page is frozen
console.log(customers) // Print customers in the console
```

With that in mind, it is easy to see why you would not like for your code to stop executing just because something is loading. That would mean that buttons will no longer work, and generally, the page would freeze.

There is a different way. You can create the function to be asynchronous and tell JavaScript not to wait for it:

```
getCustomerData().then((customerData) => {
  console.log(customerData); //would run after 4 seconds
});
allowUserToSeePhotos(); //would run immediately
```

The then() part means that you want this code to execute once the promise is returned from the other function. If needed, you can chain then() statements together, to execute them in a certain order. You can also chain into the promise a way to catch errors, and a code to execute at the end, regardless of whether the code ran successfully or failed.

```
getCustomerData()
.then((customerData) => {
  console.log(customerData);
})
.then((customerData) => { //runs after the first 'then' block
  getCreditCardInformation(customerData.emailAddress)
})
.catch((err) => console.error(err.message))//print Error
.finally(() => { //always runs at the end
    connection.close()
});
```

Promises are probably the most complicated part of JavaScript, as well as one of the most commonly used features. Do not worry too much if you do not understand everything at this particular moment. It will take some time, but you will get the hang of things. You just need to have some patience, and practice it a few times.

Summary

JavaScript is a complicated language. Everybody knows that. We all struggle with JavaScript, from beginners to senior developers. It is because it is so versatile and has so much history that it looks complicated. But with enough experience, I promise you that it all starts to make sense. You just need to have the patience to get over the first few challenges.

CHAPTER 5

The Backend

The *backend* is the part of the application that happens entirely inside of the server. This is the part that holds the information needed to run the website, the part that processes it, and that displays it for the users. The backend is the system that remembers your data, even if you log in from a different machine, and that informs you about your friend's updates on your feed page, about new job postings, or about events around your area.

The Setup (Optional)

Note If, during the setup, you encounter any issues, feel free to simply clone the Git repository at the end of the chapter and continue with the lesson.

Setting up a project can be notoriously difficult, and has a single upside, namely that it only has to be done once. To be honest, it is perfectly okay to look for a project on GitHub and start from there. If you get stuck or lost, go to the end of the chapter and download the project that's already been set up from the link. That being said, it's time to set up your backend.

In terms of programming languages, you will build the app using TypeScript, which basically a more rigid version of JavaScript. It will enable you to have access to more advanced tools for your code, and it will provide you with a lot more control over the code. But this is the reason that your files will be in the format `myFile.ts` and not `myFile.js`.

© Radu Nicoara 2023
R. Nicoara, *How to be a Web Developer*, https://doi.org/10.1007/978-1-4842-9663-9_5

Although, honestly, this project would not look that different using plain JavaScript. Modern-day web development requires TypeScript for almost all large applications, so I think it is a good idea to get accustomed to TypeScript directly, where you can.

You will be building the backend part of your application using Node. js. As a result, the first step is to install Node.js. To do that, go to `nodejs.org` and download the package from the Download section, which you should then install.

Once that is done, create a new project by following these steps:

1. Open a console by going into Windows. In the search at the bottom left, type `cmd`.

2. Create a new folder called `CRM` with the `mkdir CRM` command.

3. Navigate into the folder with `cd CRM` and create a new folder called `backend`: `mkdir backend`.

4. Go into the `backend` folder. It is time to create your node project. Do so by typing `npm init -y`, where the `-y` at the end will default all of the setup questions.

5. In order to develop your application, you have to install a few packages. Run the following commands inside of your command line:

   a. `npm install @types/express express-graphql graphql` This is the package for server-related functionality and input/output.

   b. `npm install mysql` This is needed for a MySQL connection.

c. npm install typeorm reflect-metadata You
    need this for mapping between the backend
    and MySQL.

d. npm install typescript ts-node @types/node
    This enables you to write TypeScript.

Because node is optimized for JavaScript, but you will be running
TypeScript, you need to do a few other things in addition to the initial
setup. Do not worry if you get an error during this step, and feel free to
Google any issues you encounter. You just need to edit some static text files.

Also, since these are the final steps for the setup, do not worry too
much about what they all mean. If the setup works correctly, you will
never come back to this code. You are simply following the steps in the
documentation.

Open the file called package.json and add the following scripts to it:

```
"scripts": {
  "start": "ts-node index.ts",
  "build": "tsc"
},
```

This will enable you to type npm start into your console, and that will
run your program.

Since TypeScript needs some configuration of its own, you now need
to create a file called tsconfig.json and add the following to it:

```
{
  "compilerOptions": {
    "lib": ["es5", "es6", "DOM"],
    "target": "es5",
    "module": "commonjs",
    "moduleResolution": "node",
    "outDir": "./build",
    "emitDecoratorMetadata": true,
```

```
    "experimentalDecorators": true,
    "sourceMap": true,
    "types": ["node"]
  }
}
```

Once again, do not worry too much at the moment about what all that these commands do. They are part of the documentation, and to be honestly, I myself could not tell you without searching for them.

Now that you are done with the platform setup, it is time to start building your app. In the backend folder, create a file called index.ts, which will hold the following code:

```
import express = require("express");
const app = express();
import schema from "./schema/schema";
import { graphqlHTTP } from "express-graphql";
// above are just imports of libraries and files

app.use(
  "/graphql", // the URL that we will access
  graphqlHTTP({
    schema, // the place where we will define our queries and
    mutations
    graphiql: true, // automatically provide us with a UI
  })
);

app.listen(3000, () => {
  console.log("Server is running at port 3000");
});
```

Running this code will start an application, open a port, and enable you to connect to the GraphQL endpoint. As you can see in Figure 5-1, this is just the basic configuration of what should be accessible.

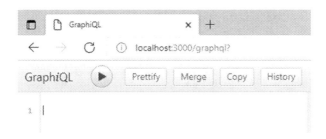

Figure 5-1. *Mapping the settings in the UI*

After you are done with the initial application, you create a folder called schema and, inside the folder, create a file called schema.ts. This is where you will define your queries and mutations, and how exactly they are going to behave. You also need to define what the objects that you are returning look like, and how they link to each other.

```
import graphql = require("graphql"); // import of the
GraphQL library
const { GraphQLObjectType, GraphQLSchema } = graphql;

const RootQuery = new GraphQLObjectType({
  name: "RootQueryType",
  fields: {}, // here, we will later add our queries
});

const schema = new GraphQLSchema({
  query: RootQuery,
});

export default schema; // export here, so we can import it in
the index.ts file
```

You can now go into your console and start the GraphQL server:

```
npm start
```

Then access http://localhost:3000/graphql (see Figure 5-2).

Figure 5-2. *Running GraphQL in Node.js*

Homework

Set up your own backend:

1. Follow the instructions in the previous section.

2. If you encounter any issues, you can find the full-working setup at https://github.com/nicoara01/ CRM/tree/main/5.1/backend.

Your First Query

In order to start developing your first query, you need to figure out exactly what you are trying to get from the database. For this first example, it will be a query that retrieves a list of all of the customers, without connecting to the database. You will go through the database connection process later. For now, you just return some static, dummy data.

That being said, you need to first create the query. Go into the ./schema/schema.ts file (./ means the current folder and ../ means the parent folder, or one folder above). Then add the following text:

```
import graphql = require("graphql");
const {
  GraphQLString,
  GraphQLID,
  GraphQLList,
  GraphQLObjectType,
  GraphQLSchema,
} = graphql;
```

```
// each object that we want to display, needs a type
declaration
const CustomerType = new GraphQLObjectType({
  name: "Customer",
  fields: () => ({ // we list all possible fields, and
  their type
    id: { type: GraphQLID },
    name: { type: GraphQLString },
    address: { type: GraphQLString },
    dateCreated: { type: GraphQLString },
  }),
});

const RootQuery = new GraphQLObjectType({
  name: "RootQueryType",
  fields: {
    getCustomers: { // the name of the query
      type: new GraphQLList(CustomerType),
      args: {},
      resolve(parent, args) {
        return [ // we just return a static array
          {
            id: 1,
            name: "Customer1",
            address: "Park Avenue 71",
            createdDate: "01-Jan-2022",
          },
        ];
      },
    },
  },
});
```

```
const schema = new GraphQLSchema({
  query: RootQuery,
});

export default schema;
```

Now you can write the query, and it will retrieve the data that you provided (see Figure 5-3).

Figure 5-3. *Running your first query in the user interface*

You can later use this data in the frontend to display a list of customers. You will develop that part of the application in the next chapter.

Note   When calling a query, the part at the beginning that surrounds the query code (query getCustomers) is placed in that location so you can reference the query later. You can name that part of the query anything you want, as it enables you to have multiple queries running into the same backend point.

Setting Up the ORM

An *ORM* (object–relational mapping) is a technique through which you create an abstraction of the database layer. But what does that mean?

Imagine that inside of your backend, you want to retrieve all of the customers from your database and provide them to your GraphQL endpoint. You would have to connect to the database and execute a query like this:

```
SELECT * FROM customer
```

But such an approach would lead to a number of problems. What will happen if you later have to change the database, and with that change, the languages will change as well? Do you rewrite the entire backend? Also, how exactly do you connect to the database? And how can you edit all of the customers using JavaScript?

For all of that, you use an ORM, which takes care of all of those problems for you. With such an approach, you only have to write code like this:

```
connection.manager.find(Customer)
```

Of course, in such simple cases, it looks to be relatively the same amount of work. But things get a lot easier with an ORM once the complexity of the code starts to increase. That is why an ORM is an absolute must in any modern web application.

In order to set up the ORM, you need to create a file called `ormconfig.json` in the backend folder. In this file, you declare which folders will contain your entities (which will map to your tables) and add the username and password details for the database.

```
{
  "type": "mysql",
  "host": "localhost",
  "port": 3306,
  "username": "root",
```

```
    "password": "",
    "database": "crm",
    "entities": ["entity/*.ts"], //what our files look like
    "cli": {
        "entitiesDir": "entity" //name of the ORM folder
    }
}
```

In the next step, you need to define the data model. You need to tell the ORM which tables it needs to connect to, and what data to pull out of them.

Inside of the backend folder, create a new folder called entity, as you defined in the last rows of your configuration file. You will add all of your entities to this folder. These entities will mostly map one-to-one to the tables (one entity per table). In this folder, create a new file called customer.ts:

```
import { Entity, PrimaryGeneratedColumn, Column } from
"typeorm"; //framework imports

@Entity("customer")
export class Customer {
    @PrimaryGeneratedColumn()
    id: number;

    @Column()
    name: string;

    @Column()
    address: string;

    @Column({ type: "date" })
    dateCreated: string;
}
```

Note the *decorator* (the part that starts with an @ symbol) before every property, which tells the ORM which parts map to what.

Now that you have set up the connection to the database and the entity mapping into the table, it is time to create a function that will retrieve the data and feed it into your GraphQL framework.

Inside the backend folder, create a new folder called service. In the service folder, create a file called characterService.ts.

Note It's a good idea to put all of the application logic in what is called the service layer. This is the part of the application that will connect to the DB layer and process the data, before serving it to the GraphQL presenter. All of the files that contain such logic will be held in the service folder.

```
import "reflect-metadata";
import { createConnection, SimpleConsoleLogger } from
"typeorm";
import { Customer } from "../entity/customer";

export async function getCustomers() {
  return createConnection()
    .then(async (connection) => { // after connection is
    created, continue
      const customers = await connection.manager.
      find(Customer); // get all customers
      connection.close(); // close connection, as we don't need
      it anymore

      return customers;
    })
    .catch((error) => console.log(error)); // log an error if
    we find one
}
```

Note the `async` definition inside of the functions. This is the major advantage of using Node.js, which is that while the process waits for the database to fetch the data, it does not stop execution, but allows other processes to run at the same time. This type of parallelism makes Node.js a great choice for large software applications with lots of users accessing them at the same time.

You now need to restart the application, so the new code will be compiled and executed. Running the query again, you will see that the data that you receive is different from what you had before:

```
npm start
```

As a result of these changes, you now have data pulling directly from the database and offering you a list of all the customers that you added to the database (see Figure 5-4).

Figure 5-4. *Running the first program that connects to the database*

Homework

Set up your own backend to interact with the database:

1. Make sure that your XAMPP is running.

2. Follow the previous instructions.

3. If you encounter any issues, you can find the full-working setup at https://github.com/nicoara01/CRM/tree/main/5.2/backend.

Your First Mutation

A mutation, in the context of GraphQL, is a way to create, edit, or delete data on the server side. You will therefore need to develop a mutation that will create a new customer. You then can see the newly added data when using the previously built query.

The mutation will need to take in as input the name and address fields and insert that data as a new row in the database. The ID and dateCreated fields will automatically be generated (see Figure 5-5).

***Figure 5-5.** Data flow in GraphQL*

This is relatively easy to do, since you have it all set up. Open the .schema/schema.ts file and add the following code:

```
...
const RootMutation = new GraphQLObjectType({
  name: "RootMutationType",
  fields: {
    createCustomer: {
      type: CustomerType, //return the newly created customer
      args: { name: { type: GraphQLString }, address: { type:
      GraphQLString } }, //we take the name and address as
      arguments/inputs
      resolve(parent, args) {
        return createCustomer(args.name, args.address);
      },
    },
  },
});
```

```
const schema = new GraphQLSchema({
  query: RootQuery,
  mutation: RootMutation,
});

export default schema;
```

After this step, you need to go in the file called `./service/customerService.ts` and add the following function, which you were calling previously:

```
export async function createCustomer(name: string, address:
string) {
  return createConnection()
    .then(async (connection) => {
      const customer = new Customer();
      customer.name = name;
      customer.address = address;
      customer.dateCreated = new Date().toLocaleDateString
      ("en-CA");//in the format YYYY-MM-DD

      await connection.manager.save(customer);

      connection.close();

      return customer;
    })
    .catch((error) => console.log(error)); //catch any error
}
```

That is mostly it. When you call the mutation, you will create a new Customer object, and then you will set the fields that you are interested in, save them using the ORM, and return the object, together with the ID that you just inserted in the database.

You simply need to restart Node.js using npm start and you'll be finished (see Figure 5-6).

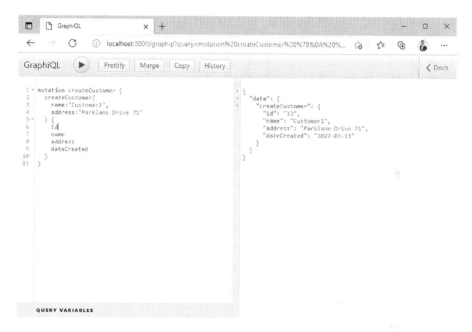

Figure 5-6. *Calling a mutation*

Homework

Set up your own backend to interact with the database:

1. Follow the previous instructions to create your mutation.

2. If you encounter any issues, you can find the full-working setup at https://github.com/nicoara01/CRM/tree/main/6.3/backend.

Summary

This chapter explained how to the set up and develop the backend section of your application. You also read an overview of the various components that make up a modern backend application. In addition to this, you learned about the way that data flows in and out of the system, using GraphQL queries and mutations.

There are, of course, a large number of features, tests, and configurations that involve making such a system production-ready. But the aim of this chapter is to give you enough information and examples, so that you can continue to explore the beautiful world of backend development on your own.

CHAPTER 6

The Frontend

The frontend is the part of an application that simply brings it to life. It is the interface through which the users interact with all of the functionalities being offered to them. It is no secret that for me personally, the frontend is my favorite part of web development. There are so many things to build in the frontend and so many to improve—so many tiny design decisions that are instantly visible to the end users and so many user experience concepts that can be implemented. Because of its high visibility, the frontend is also the part that needs the most maintenance.

For any application, a backend that is ten years old, if initially built correctly, will most likely continuously work without needing to be touched. But designs change every two-three years, so that means that your frontend needs to stay in line with the times.

Frontend development as a concept can seem contradictory. On the one hand, it is the part of web development that is the most complicated. It always needs new frameworks and new libraries, and it is generally cumbersome and has a steep learning curve.

But do not let that fool you! The frontend is also the part that feels the least like programming. You constantly have to talk to the users and representatives, brainstorm for designs, gather feedback, and generally be prepared to do all types of adjacent tasks in relation to programming. This chapter looks at what exactly the frontend is in a modern application.

© Radu Nicoara 2023
R. Nicoara, *How to be a Web Developer*, https://doi.org/10.1007/978-1-4842-9663-9_6

The Figma UX/UI

The first step to creating any application is to determine what exactly you need to display, and how exactly your users will interact with the application.

Since, in the backend, you only have a list of clients and the possibility to create a new client, you need to build a user interface related to this functionality. When building a new UI, it is perfectly okay to start with a wireframe, just to throw some ideas around. A professional UI designer will build a UI proposal in software like *Figma*. This is a free online UX/UI tool that can be found at figma.com.

Inside of Figma, you can create a new web project, where you will use simple rectangles and text to create a basic UI sketch of what you need to achieve.

Some argue that you can use rectangles and text, even in Microsoft Word, to achieve the same result. But Figma offers you the opportunity to use the same components that you will use in React, so you can create a pretty accurate UI representation of what the frontend is going to look like.

Besides that, Figma offers you the possibility to create multiple screens and link them through click actions, so that you can create a pseudo-application that is much easier to test with your users.

But for this case, it is enough to simply create a quick sketch in Figma so that you can then proceed to building your frontend (see Figure 6-1).

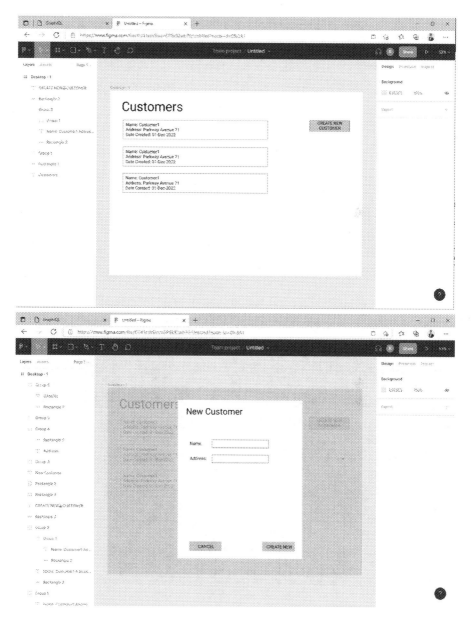

Figure 6-1. *Two pages of the Figma UX design*

There is no need, at the current time and for your current application, to set up a complicated project, so that you can validate it with your users. A short sketch will do just fine, for now. But note the design that you just made, as you will learn to implement it in React in the following chapters.

The Setup

You will be building your frontend application using React, so the first step is to set up the project. In order to do that, go to the command line and navigate to the crm folder. Then you just run the command to create a new React project. This command will also create a new folder:

```
npx create-react-app frontend
```

Then, if you change the directory to the new frontend folder, you can see all of your files (see Figure 6-2).

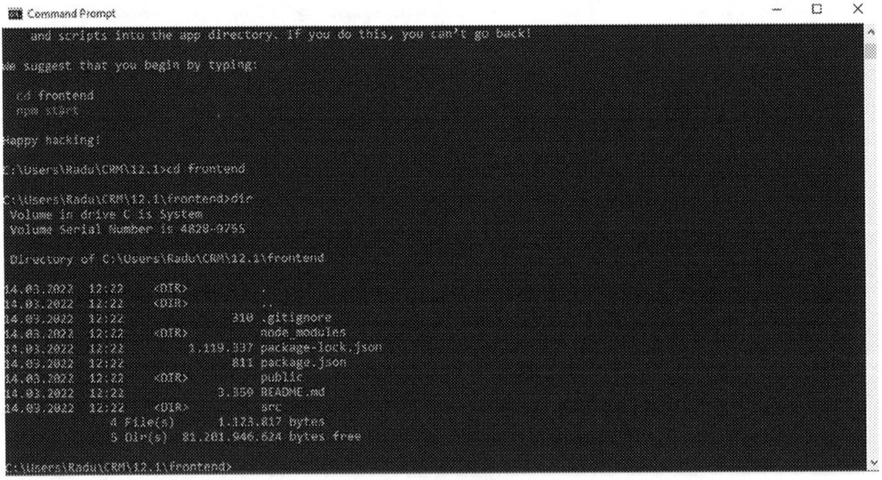

Figure 6-2. *Creating your frontend setup*

You have node_modules, where the node just automatically downloads the libraries it needs, and the package files, which only contain the node requirements. The important part of the application is found in the src folder, but there is no need to go there just yet. You first need to test that it all went well.

In order to do that, you can simply run npm start to start your application. Once you see the default landing page of your application (see Figure 6-3), you know you are ready to start developing your application.

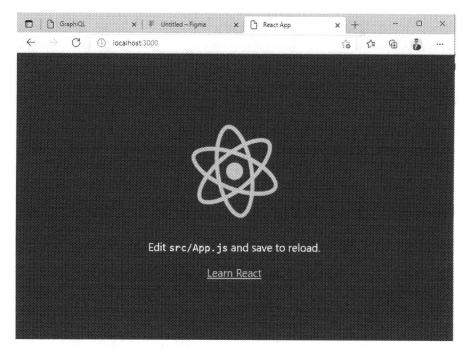

Figure 6-3. Landing page of the default React application

The Static Page

The first part of developing a CRM application is making the page look like the one in your Figma design, only without any functionality. (You will add the functionality later.)

Go to ./frontend/src/App.js and bring it to its bare bones:

```
import './App.css';

function App() {
  return (
    <div>

    </div>
  );
}

export default App;
```

Then, inside of this file, add a header as the title and a div containing the details related to your clients.

```
function App() {
  return (
    <div>
      <h2>Clients</h2>
      <div className="client_border">
        <p>
          Name: <b>Client1</b>
        </p>
        <p>
          Address: <b>Park Avenue 71</b>
        </p>
        <p>
          Date Created: <b>01-Dec-2022</b>
        </p>
      </div>
    </div>
  );
}
```

Note that in React, the word `class` is reserved, so use the keyword `className` as an attribute, in order to provide a rendered element with a class.

Then go into the `App.css` file and delete everything, so that you can add the CSS for your app:

```
.client_border {
  border: 1px solid black;
}
```

If you open your browser now, you can see how the app currently looks when it's being accessed (see Figure 6-4).

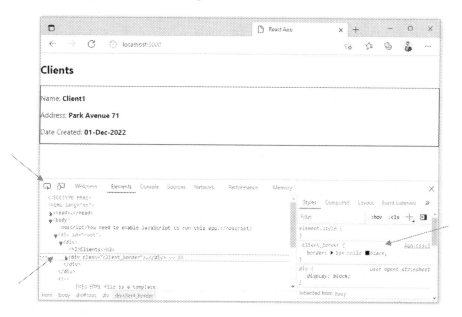

Figure 6-4. *Using the browser console*

As a note, in order to inspect the CSS, right-click the browser window, then go to Inspect. Using the Select an Element on the Page to Inspect It option, select your `client_border` div to view its CSS. This will display the rendered HTML elements and the CSS properties for each of them.

If you now look at your Figma design, you can see that you have two columns. One for the clients and one for the button. The current design only holds each element to have 100 percent width. This is a perfect moment to bring Bootstrap into the picture.

Bootstrap enables you to add better CSS to everything and provides you with access to a large number of prebuilt React components.

Head to `react-bootstrap.github.io` and install the node library according to the instructions there. It is as easy as simply running the npm `install react-bootstrap bootstrap` command and then restarting your frontend server. (The URL will have a large number of examples in the documentation.)

Now, going to the documentation, you can see that you need to simply add a `<row>` and `<col>` element to achieve your layout (see Figure 6-5).

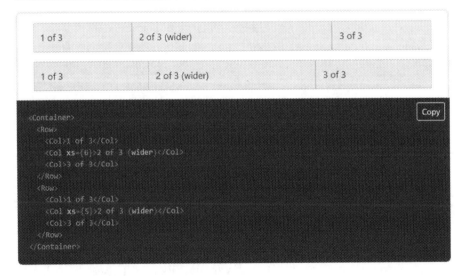

Setting one column width

Auto-layout for flexbox grid columns also means you can set the width of one column and have the sibling columns automatically resize around it. You may use predefined grid classes (as shown below), grid mixins, or inline widths. Note that the other columns will resize no matter the width of the center column.

| 1 of 3 | 2 of 3 (wider) | 3 of 3 |
| 1 of 3 | 2 of 3 (wider) | 3 of 3 |

```
<Container>
  <Row>
    <Col>1 of 3</Col>
    <Col xs={6}>2 of 3 (wider)</Col>
    <Col>3 of 3</Col>
  </Row>
  <Row>
    <Col>1 of 3</Col>
    <Col xs={5}>2 of 3 (wider)</Col>
    <Col>3 of 3</Col>
  </Row>
</Container>
```

Figure 6-5. *Documentation of React Bootstrap*

You can also go into the documentation to find a button that you can use to create the customer.

This now brings you to the following code for your `./frontend/src/App.js`:

```
import "./App.css";
import "bootstrap/dist/css/bootstrap.min.css"; // Imports CSS
import { Container, Col, Row, Button } from "react-bootstrap";
// Imports bootstrap elements

function App() {
  return (
    <Container>
      <h2>Clients</h2>
      <Row>
        <Col xs={10}>
          <div className="client_border">
            <p>
              Name: <b>Client1</b>
            </p>
            <p>
              Address: <b>Park Avenue 71</b>
            </p>
            <p>
              Date Created: <b>01-Dec-2022</b>
            </p>
          </div>
        </Col>
        <Col>
          <Button variant="primary">Create New</Button>
        </Col>
```

```
    </Row>
  </Container>
  );
}
```

```
export default App;
```

As you can see, the page does not contain any dynamic text, meaning that you cannot currently influence the way the page looks just by the code (see Figure 6-6). You will add this functionality a bit later.

Figure 6-6. *The static web page*

Creating the Popup

You now need to create a popup in such a way that, when you click the Create New button, it will come up, display on top of the entire background web page, and prompt you to provide the data you need to create a new customer.

Looking at the Bootstrap documentation, you can see that a *modal* component will most likely provide you with all the functionality that you need. And that is out of the box, and with no necessary changes. See Figure 6-7.

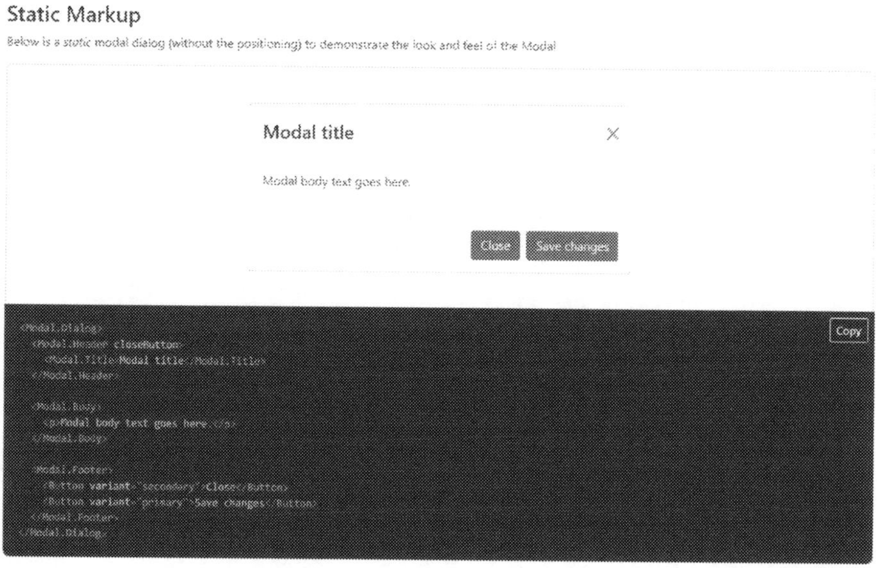
Static Markup
Below is a static modal dialog (without the positioning) to demonstrate the look and feel of the Modal
Modal title
Modal body text goes here.
Close
Save changes
Copy

Figure 6-7. *The modal component*

The only problem is that you need to know when to display the modal and when not to. Since you cannot have the modal always on, you need to know when the button was clicked, and when the modal should be closed. This brings me neatly to the moment where I need to introduce *React states.*

This is likely the most complicated part of React, and it is what makes this framework different than anything else. So what exactly are states? How do they work, and how are they different?

States are variables that are controlled by the framework. They can only be set or changed by using the setter functions, and whenever you change them, the change is asynchronous, meaning it will not happen instantly, but at a certain point in the future.

The first step to using a state is to import the function from the framework:

```
import { useState } from "react";
```

Then, you declare the state like this:

```
const [isModalVisible, setIsModalVisible] = useState(false);
```

This means that you will have a variable called isModalVisible and a function called setIsModalVisible. The default value of the variable will be false because that is the value provided as a parameter to the useState function.

Now, just to test your code, you can write a paragraph that will be displayed only if this variable is set to true.

```
{isModalVisible && <p>Only visible in modal</p>}
```

Okay. There are a lot of things happening in the previous lines of code, so let's get a bit more into the JavaScript and see what is actually happening.

Destructuring is a procedure in JavaScript by which you can take an object with multiple attributes and push those into separate variables. This is covered in Chapter 10.

Therefore, when you write:

```
import { useState } from "react";
```

This means that the module called react exports a list of multiple properties, out of which you only need the useState one.

Using a variable and the && sign means that if the variable resolves as true, continue reading the code, but if it is false, stop the execution and move on. It is basically a short, condensed if/else.

Now it is time to return to the popup modal:

```
import "./App.css";
import "bootstrap/dist/css/bootstrap.min.css"; // Imports CSS
for bootstrap
import { Container, Col, Row, Button, Modal } from "react-
bootstrap"; // Imports bootstrap elements
```

```
import { useState } from "react"; // Import state from React

function App() {
  const [isModalVisible, setIsModalVisible] = useState(false);

  return (
    <Container>
      <h2>Clients</h2>
      <Row>
        <Col xs={10}>
          <div className="client_border">
            <p>
              Name: <b>Client1</b>
            </p>
            <p>
              Address: <b>Park Avenue 71</b>
            </p>
            <p>
              Date Created: <b>01-Dec-2022</b>
            </p>
          </div>
        </Col>
        <Col>
          <Button variant="primary" onClick={() =>
          setIsModalVisible(true)}>
            Create New
          </Button>
        </Col>
      </Row>
```

```
      <Modal
        show={isModalVisible}
        onHide={() => {
          // we simply call the setter with the new value, when
          closing the modal
          setIsModalVisible(false);
        }}
      >
        <Modal.Header closeButton>
          <Modal.Title>Create New Customer</Modal.Title>
        </Modal.Header>

        <Modal.Body>
          <p>Modal body text goes here.</p>
        </Modal.Body>

        <Modal.Footer>
          <Button
            variant="secondary"
            onClick={() => {
              setIsModalVisible(false);
            }}
          >
            Close
          </Button>
          <Button variant="primary">Save changes</Button>
        </Modal.Footer>
      </Modal>
    </Container>
  );
}

export default App;
```

After you click the Create New button, your application will look like Figure 6-8.

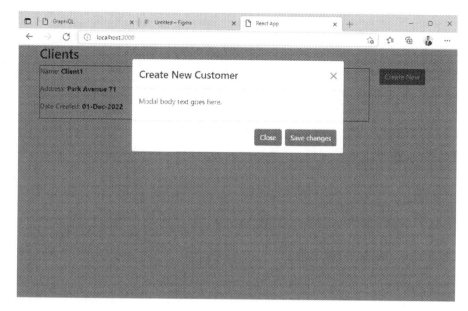

Figure 6-8. *The popup that you built*

The best part of using states in React is that when a state is updated, the framework will calculate what type of changes need to be made, in order for the web page to be brought to the new state. Then React will only perform those minimal changes.

This is the reason that, by using React, you can start building *single page applications*. Because you won't need to refresh the page every time you need to pull some new data in. You don't redirect users to new pages; instead you display everything on a single page.

Homework (30-40 Min)

Set up your own frontend:

1. Follow the previous instructions to create your frontend.

2. If you encounter any issues, you can find the full-working setup at `https://github.com/nicoara01/CRM/tree/main/6.1/frontend`.

Creating React Components

Once you start to add functionality to the `App.js` file, you can easily see how the file could become unmanageable. You cannot simply add code infinitely to a single file, so you need a way to split things up. This is exactly the place where React shines. You will move the entire modal into a separate component and provide the state as a parameter to the new component.

Create a new file called `CreateCustomer.js` and place the new code for your component:

```
// Import bootstrap elements
import { Button, Modal } from "react-bootstrap";
function CreateCustomer({ isModalVisible,
setIsModalVisible }) {
  return <Modal
    show={isModalVisible}
    onHide={() => {
        setIsModalVisible(false);
    }}
    >
  <Modal.Header closeButton>
    <Modal.Title>Create New Customer</Modal.Title>
  </Modal.Header>
```

```
<Modal.Body>
  <p>Modal body text goes here.</p>
</Modal.Body>

<Modal.Footer>
  <Button
    variant="secondary"
    onClick={() => {
      setIsModalVisible(false);
    }}
  >
    Close
  </Button>
  <Button variant="primary">Save changes</Button>
</Modal.Footer>
</Modal>
}
```

```
export default CreateCustomer
```

Now, you just need to go into the App.js and import the new component in the head.

```
import CreateCustomer from "./CreateCustomer";
```

Then call it with the proper parameters, replacing the previous modal code, which is now found in the new file.

```
<CreateCustomer
    isModalVisible={isModalVisible}
    setIsModalVisible={setIsModalVisible}
/>
```

Therefore, the entire modal part will be executed separately.

Homework (10 Min)

Split up the App.js file on your own:

1. Follow the previous instructions to create your
   frontend.

2. If you encounter any issues, you can find the full-
   working setup at https://github.com/nicoara01/
   CRM/tree/main/6.3/frontend.

Linking the Backend and the Frontend Using Apollo

Since you need to run the frontend and the backend in parallel, you need
to change the port that the backend runs on, as at the moment they both
will try to connect to port 3000. That means one will always fail.

Therefore, go to ./backend/index.ts and change the port to 3100:

```
app.listen(3100, () => {
  console.log("Server is running at port 3100");
});
```

Another thing you need to do is enable *CORS* (cross-origin resource
sharing). CORS allows you to safely communicate between your frontend
and your backend. Basically, the frontend of an application generally
only tries to communicate to a backend in the same domain, mostly for
security purposes. Since your website is running on localhost, and that
is not a registered domain, your browser might not want to connect to
the backend. In order to fix this, you need to install the CORS package
and use it:

```
npm install cors
```

Then, add the following to ./backend/index.ts:

```
import cors from "cors";
app.use(cors());
```

This will make your file in ./backend/index.ts look like this:

```
import express = require("express");
const app = express();
import schema from "./schema/schema";
import { graphqlHTTP } from "express-graphql";
import cors from "cors";

app.use(cors());
app.use(
  "/graphql", // the URL that we will access
  graphqlHTTP({
    schema, // the place where we will define our queries and
    mutations
    graphiql: true, // automatically provide us with a UI
  })
);

app.listen(3100, () => {
  console.log("Server is running at port 3100");
});
```

You need to have two command lines open, one for each process. So, for the backend, you can simply launch the application.

In order to connect to the backend using GraphQL, you need to *instantiate* the Apollo library, so you follow the documentation steps from https://www.apollographql.com/docs/react/get-started/

In order to run Apollo on the frontend, you need to run the following command in the `frontend` folder:

```
npm install @apollo/client graphql
```

Now add the library to `.frontend/index.js` and then pass it to all the child elements:

```
import React from "react";
import ReactDOM from "react-dom";
import "./index.css";
import App from "./App";
import reportWebVitals from "./reportWebVitals";
import { ApolloClient, InMemoryCache, ApolloProvider } from
"@apollo/client";

const client = new ApolloClient({
  uri: "http://localhost:3100/graphql",
  cache: new InMemoryCache(),
});

ReactDOM.render(
  <React.StrictMode>
    <ApolloProvider client={client}>
      <App />
    </ApolloProvider>
  </React.StrictMode>,
  document.getElementById("root")
);
reportWebVitals();
```

This takes you to your App.js file:

```
import "./App.css";
import "bootstrap/dist/css/bootstrap.min.css"; // Imports CSS
for bootstrap
import { Container, Col, Row, Button } from "react-bootstrap";
// Imports bootstrap elements
import { useState } from "react"; // import state from React
import CreateCustomer from "./CreateCustomer";
import { useQuery, gql } from "@apollo/client";

const GET_CUSTOMERS_QUERY = gql`
  query getCustomers {
    getCustomers {
      id
      name
      address
      dateCreated
    }
  }
`;

function App() {
  const [isModalVisible, setIsModalVisible] = useState(false);
  const { loading, error, data } = useQuery(GET_
  CUSTOMERS_QUERY);

  return (
    <Container>
      <h2>Clients</h2>
      <Row>
        <Col xs={10}>
          {data &&
```

```
            data.getCustomers.map((client) => {
              return (
                <div className="client_border">
                  <p>
                    Name: <b>{client.name}</b>
                  </p>
                  <p>
                    Address: <b>{client.address}</b>
                  </p>
                  <p>
                    Date Created: <b>{client.dateCreated}</b>
                  </p>
                </div>
              );
            })}
        </Col>
        <Col>
          <Button variant="primary" onClick={() =>
          setIsModalVisible(true)}>
            Create New
          </Button>
        </Col>
      </Row>
      <CreateCustomer
        isModalVisible={isModalVisible}
        setIsModalVisible={setIsModalVisible}
      />
    </Container>
  );
}

export default App;
```

As you can now see, importing from the Apollo library will give you three variables: a `loading` variable, which is set to `true` when the data is loading, an `error` variable, which is normally `null`, but will contain an error in the eventuality that you receive one, and a `data` variable, where the result of your query is stored. You then run a `map` function over the data, and that will create a `div` element for each customer in your database (see Figure 6-9).

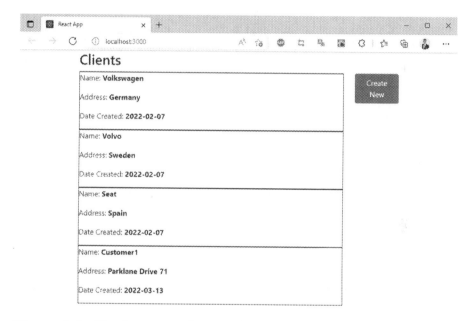

Figure 6-9. *The React app listing clients*

If you open the console in your browser, you can see the network call to the backend, and the data that came back. Just right-click the page and choose Inspect. Then go to the Network page (see Figure 6-10).

Figure 6-10. *Inspecting the app*

Also, in order to debug your React code, you can install an extension for React in your browser. Just search for "React Developer Tools" in your browser's extension page and install them. This will give you access to a new tab, where you can see the states of each component that you built (see Figure 6-11).

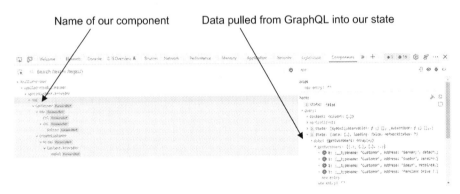

Figure 6-11. *Details of the app inspection*

Using Mutations to Create a Customer

Now that you have the entre popup modal inside a separate component, you will add three inputs. When the users click Create, your code will call the mutation with the provided data.

But first, you need to add a new property to the query in App.js, so that you have a function that fetches the query on your command. You will then call this function after you push a mutation, so you always display the latest data from the database.

```
const {
  loading,
  error,
  data,
  refetch: refetchQuery,
} = useQuery(GET_CUSTOMERS_QUERY);
```

You will then provide this new function as a parameter when you render your component:

```
<CreateCustomer
  isModalVisible={isModalVisible}
  setIsModalVisible={setIsModalVisible}
  // It is up to us what we name this parameter
  refetchQuery={refetchQuery} />
```

Then your CreateCustomer.js file will look like this:

```
import { Button, Modal, Form } from "react-bootstrap";
// Imports bootstrap elements
import { useState } from "react"; // import state from React
import { useMutation, gql } from "@apollo/client";

const CREATE_CUSTOMER_MUTATION = gql`
  mutation createCustomer($name: String, $address: String) {
    createCustomer(name: $name, address: $address) {
      id
    }
  }
`;
```

```
function CreateCustomer({ isModalVisible, setIsModalVisible,
refetchQuery }) {
  const [customerName, setCustomerName] = useState("");
  const [customerAddress, setCustomerAddress] = useState("");

  const [createCustomerMutation] = useMutation(CREATE_CUSTOMER_
  MUTATION);

  const saveCustomer = () => { // called when we click
  save button
    createCustomerMutation({
      variables: {
        name: customerName,
        address: customerAddress,
      },
    }).then(() => {
      // reset data, and close modal
      refetchQuery();
      setCustomerName("");
      setCustomerAddress("");
      setIsModalVisible(false);
    });
  };

  return (
    <Modal
      show={isModalVisible}
      onHide={() => {
        // we simply call the setter with the new value as a
        parameter
        setIsModalVisible(false);
      }}
    >
```

```
<Modal.Header closeButton>
  <Modal.Title>Create New Customer</Modal.Title>
</Modal.Header>

<Modal.Body>
  Name
  <Form.Control
    value={customerName}
    onChange={(e) => setCustomerName(e.target.value)}
    // e is here an event, so we get the value of the
    change event
  />
  Address
  <Form.Control
    value={customerAddress}
    onChange={(e) => setCustomerAddress(e.target.value)}
  />
</Modal.Body>

<Modal.Footer>
  <Button
    variant="secondary"
    onClick={() => {
      setIsModalVisible(false);
    }}
  >
    Close
  </Button>
  <Button variant="primary" onClick={saveCustomer}>
    Save changes
```

```
        </Button>
      </Modal.Footer>
    </Modal>
  );
}

export default CreateCustomer;
```

All of these changes will lead to a modal like the one in Figure 6-12, once you click the button to create a new customer. Saving the customer will call the mutation, which in turn, will save the data to your database.

Figure 6-12. *The Create New Customer popup*

Homework

Set up the connection between your backend and your frontend:

1. Follow the previous instructions to set up both the backend and the frontend.

2. If you encounter any issues, you can find the full-working setup at `https://github.com/nicoara01/CRM/tree/main/6.3/frontend`.

Summary

In this chapter, you learned how to build a modern frontend solution using React and Bootstrap, and how to connect it to a backend system using Apollo. The most important part of building a modern frontend system is choosing a framework, and at the moment, React is your best bet.

I encourage you to take some time and go through the homework in this chapter. Even try to expand the application a little bit. The main purpose of this chapter was to offer you the fundamentals of frontend development, and it is entirely up to you to discover more about the particularities of JavaScript and React.

After all, a modern backend system can only transmit some JSON encoded data, and it is up to a skilled frontend developer (hopefully you!) to transform that long JSON data into a well-rounded and user-friendly application.

CHAPTER 7

Going Fullstack

In the last chapter, you left your system with the following features: the ability to list all the customers inside the database, and, with the help of a popup, the ability to create a new user. The application currently looks like Figure 7-1.

Figure 7-1. *The current state of your application*

Now imagine that your Project Manager assigned to you two tickets that you need to finish by the end of the week. These tickets are:

1. **Make a better design.** The users have complained that even though the system works as it should, it does not look pretty. You need to make the system look more "modern."

© Radu Nicoara 2023
R. Nicoara, *How to be a Web Developer*, https://doi.org/10.1007/978-1-4842-9663-9_7

2. **Add the ability to delete customers.** One user created a customer by mistake, and they want to be able to delete it. You need to provide the ability to delete customers, in addition to creating them.

With these two tickets assigned to your name, you are now officially a fullstack developer. Hooray! The next sections explain how to achieve what your team needs from you, as well as how to deliver what your customers request from you.

The Design Ticket

The problem of design, in the field of web development, is that everybody has an opinion about how it should be done. Since there is no single objective way to create a "good design," this can easily lead to an unproductive state, where everybody is simply trying to push their own vision.

In order to avoid that, the best way to go about the design phase is to have a single person responsible for it, and luckily for this project, that person is you. Now, in order to make your design more "modern," first look for some inspiration. It is even better if you find something that you can easily implement.

As a result, I head over to the React Bootstrap documentation, to see if I can find a component that I can easily reuse. As a result, you will be heading to `https://react-bootstrap.github.io` and trying to find interesting components to add to your application.

The first thing that I would add to the application is a navigation bar, since it will add a bit of space at the top and make your app look more like a website. This component will also provide navigation options, once you start expanding the tool. Fortunately, the navigation bar that Bootstrap provides might be exactly what you need, as you can see in Figure 7-2.

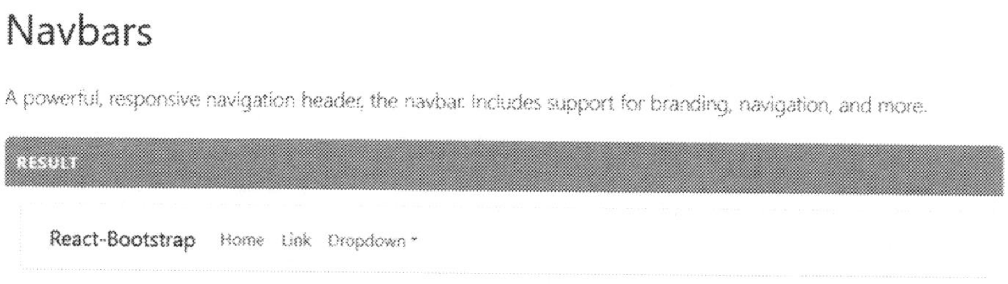

Navbars

A powerful, responsive navigation header, the navbar includes support for branding, navigation, and more.

RESULT

React-Bootstrap   Home   Link   Dropdown ▾

Figure 7-2. *The navigation bar that Bootstrap provides in the documentation page*

As a result, you will just copy/paste the code from the documentation and change the name of the links. This will meet your current navigation needs. This will make the ./frontend/src/App.js file look like the following code.

Pay attention to the fact that you are using two new Bootstrap components, namely <Navbar> and <Nav>, and as a result, you need to import them into the file.

```
import { Container, Col, Row, Button, Navbar, Nav } from
"react-bootstrap";
...
<>
    <Navbar bg="primary" data-bs-theme="dark" variant="dark">
        <Container>
          <Navbar.Brand href="/">My CRM</Navbar.Brand>
          <Nav className="me-auto">
            <Nav.Link href="/">Customers</Nav.Link>
          </Nav>
        </Container>
    </Navbar>
    <Container>
        <h2>Clients</h2>
        <Row>
          ...
</>
```

Go to the ./frontend/App.css file and add the following margin to the styling, to add a bit more space at the top:

```
h2 {
  margin: 20px 0 15px 0 !important;
}
```

With that being done, your application now looks like Figure 7-3, which is already significantly better.

Figure 7-3. *The app with a navigation bar*

But you are still left with the entire list of customers, which doesn't necessarily look pretty at all.

One idea is to list them in a table to have it at least more organized and easier to understand. Such an approach would look like Figure 7-4, and I may add that it is not too bad. To achieve such a result, Bootstrap provides a table component that is lightly stylized, making it a decent option.

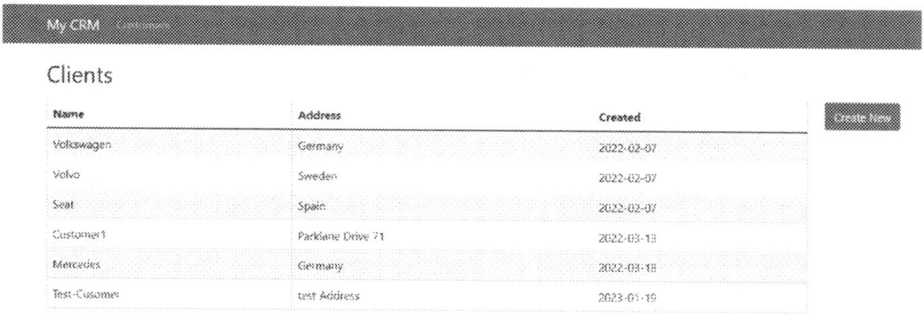

Clients

Name	Address	Created	
Volkswagen	Germany	2022-02-07	Create New
Volvo	Sweden	2022-02-07	
Seat	Spain	2022-02-07	
Customer1	Parklane Drive 71	2022-03-13	
Mercedes	Germany	2022-03-13	
Test-Cusomer	test Address	2023-01-19	

Figure 7-4. *Using tables to list all customers*

The code for such an approach is also relatively easy to implement. Just go to the Bootstrap documentation to see the types of predesigned table they offer. Then, you just use copy/paste to add that code to your application, as shown in Figure 7-5.

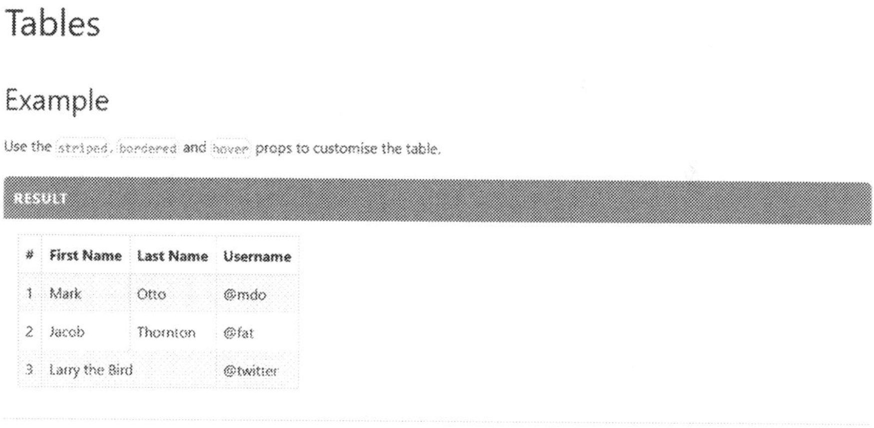

Tables

Example

Use the `striped`, `bordered` and `hover` props to customise the table.

#	First Name	Last Name	Username
1	Mark	Otto	@mdo
2	Jacob	Thornton	@fat
3	Larry the Bird		@twitter

Figure 7-5. *The table that Bootstrap has to offer to the React application*

127

That being said, you simply need to import it to use the `<Table>`
component provided by Bootstrap:

```
...
<Row>
  <Col xs={10}>
    <Table striped bordered hover>
      <thead>
        <tr>
          <th>Name</th>
          <th>Address</th>
          <th>Created</th>
        </tr>
      </thead>
      <tbody>
        {data &&
          data.getCustomers.map((client) => {
            return (
              <tr>
                <td>{client.name}</td>
                <td>{client.address}</td>
                <td>{client.dateCreated}</td>
              </tr>
            );
          })}
      </tbody>
    </Table>
  </Col>
  <Col>
    <Button variant="primary" onClick={() =>
    setIsModalVisible(true)}>
      Create New
```

```
    </Button>
  </Col>
</Row>
```

•••

The table approach does make the application look better, and you can certainly leave things like they are now. But I believe that you can do an even better job, when it comes to the design of your application. My personal approach would be to use some sort of card system to list all the customers. This would be similar to the analog business cards used in the physical world.

Again, going to Bootstrap, you find exactly what you need, from the `<Card>` component (see Figure 7-6).

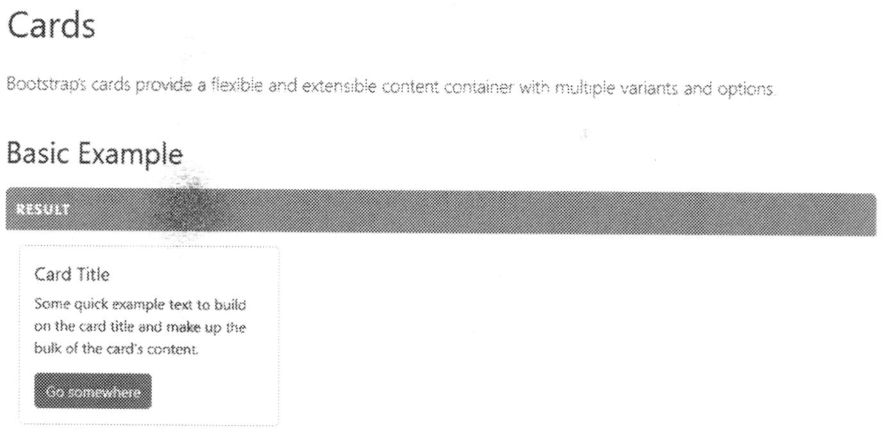

Cards

Bootstrap's cards provide a flexible and extensible content container with multiple variants and options.

Basic Example

RESULT

Card Title

Some quick example text to build on the card title and make up the bulk of the card's content.

Go somewhere

Figure 7-6. The Card component inside Bootstrap

With this component, you can now use the `.map()` function on your customer array to render one card for each customer. You will style the component a bit, and add the button to delete a customer.

```
{data &&
  data.getCustomers.map((client) => {
    return (
     <Card className="customer_card">
      <Card.Header>{client.name}</Card.Header>
      <Card.Body>
        <Card.Text>
          {client.address}
          <div className="date_created_card">
            {client.dateCreated}
          </div>
        </Card.Text>
        <Button variant="outline-danger" size="sm">
          Delete
        </Button>
      </Card.Body>
     </Card>
     );
  })}
```

You also need to add the styling in the App.css file, to make sure that
the date is smaller than the address and the button is on the right of the
card. You also need to make sure that all cards are in a line, because by
default they will render at full-width and be underneath each other.

Add the following CSS code to your application:

```
.customer_card {
  width: 300px;
  float: left;
  margin: 10px 10px 0 0;
}
```

```
.date_created_card {
  color: grey;
  font-size: 10px;
}

.customer_card button {
  float: right;
}
```

With all of that coding done, you can now see your new frontend, freshly designed for your CRM application (see Figure 7-7).

Figure 7-7. *The new design of your CRM application*

The New Feature Ticket

You were also asked to create a way for users to delete a customer from the database. In order to achieve that, you need to split the ticket into two parts:

1. The backend. Create a mutation that takes a customer ID as input and deletes it from the database.

2. The frontend. Add a button (you already did this) and write a function to call the delete mutation.

131

Start with the first part, as it makes more logical sense to start with the backend. You first need to create the function that will go in the database and delete the customer with a certain ID. You will then go to the `./backend/service/customerService.ts` file and add a function to it:

```
export async function deleteCustomer(id: number) {
  return createConnection()
    .then(async (connection) => {
      const user = await connection.manager.findOne(Customer,
      { id: id });
      await connection.manager.remove(user);
      connection.close();
    })
    .catch((error) => console.log(error));
}
```

Now build the mutation in the `./backend/schema/schema.ts` file by adding a field in the `RootMutation` object. It will call the newly created function. The new mutation does need to return something, but you will just return `true` every time. If an error occurs, it will be treated differently by the entire system.

Make sure to import `GraphQLBoolean` from GraphQL and the new function called `deleteCustomer` from `customerService.js`. Then you can add the following to your code:

```
...
const RootMutation = new GraphQLObjectType({
  name: "RootMutationType",
  fields: {
    createCustomer: {
      type: CustomerType, // return the newly created customer
      args: { name: { type: GraphQLString }, address: { type:
      GraphQLString } }, // we take the name and address
      as inputs
```

```
    resolve(parent, args) {
      return createCustomer(args.name, args.address);
    },
  },
  deleteCustomer: {
    type: GraphQLBoolean,
    args: {
      id: { type: GraphQLID},
    },
    resolve(parent, args) {
      deleteCustomer(args.id);
      return true;
    },
  },
},
});
...
```

Now go to the frontend to create a function that will call the mutation, and that will refresh the user list once you call the mutation.

First add the mutation as a string to the App.js file, then register it to the useMutation() function, which comes from the GraphQL library. After that, create a new function that will be called every time you click the button, and afterwards, you simply link the button to it:

```
...
const DELETE_CUSTOMER_MUTATION = gql`
  mutation deleteCustomer($id: ID) {
    deleteCustomer(id: $id)
  }
`;
...
```

```
const [deleteCustomerMutation] = useMutation(DELETE_CUSTOMER_
MUTATION);

const deleteCustomer = (id) => {
  deleteCustomerMutation({ variables: { id: id }
}).then(() => {
    refetchQuery();  // get back data after deletion
  });
};
...
 <Button
   variant="outline-danger"
   size="sm"
   onClick={() => {
     deleteCustomer(client.id);
   }}
 >
   Delete
</Button>
 ...
```

You will now see that when you click the Delete button on each card, the card will disappear. Your browser will refresh a new list of customers automatically (see Figure 7-8).

Figure 7-8. *The new list of customers, after the last entry has been deleted*

Homework

Implement the requirements that were presented at the beginning of the chapter:

1. Follow the instructions to improve the design and create the needed mutation.

2. Feel free to add design elements to the application, like a footer, or even a new page for contacts.

3. If you encounter any issues, you can find the full-working setup at `https://github.com/nicoara01/CRM/tree/main/7.1/`.

Summary

In this chapter, you received a list of elements and features that needed to be added to your application. For your first task as a fullstack developer, you added various Bootstrap elements to your design, and then created the mutation needed to enable users to delete a customer.

CHAPTER 8

Automated Testing

If you have finished building your application (covered in the previous chapter), you might think you are ready to hand it over to your customers. But how can you ensure that all the new features work as intended? You could always go in and start testing the application manually.

Although this is not necessarily a bad idea, and from time to time you might need to go into the app and see if it all works correctly, will you manually test the entire app every time you deploy a new feature? What about library updates or maintenance? You can see how, after a year of work, you would have hundreds of features that you would need to test on an almost daily basis.

This is the point where automated testing comes in. You can automate a large part of the testing, so that when you deploy a new feature, you'll have full confidence that you did not break anything else. Even if are trying to deploy something complex, and you do end up breaking something, you will have the confidence that you can determine in minutes what went well and what went wrong.

Testing Concepts

Testing is one of those topics in development that definitely deserves an entire chapter, and this section takes a quick look into what testing is and what you can do with it.

© Radu Nicoara 2023
R. Nicoara, *How to be a Web Developer*, https://doi.org/10.1007/978-1-4842-9663-9_8

Testing is an automated process whereby a series of prewritten testing scenarios are tested against a piece of code. These scenarios will run before or after the code is merged back into the main branch in your Git environment. But these series of tests can also be run manually, so that you can make sure that your code changes don't brake anything important.

Testing is a great way to make sure that your code does what it is supposed to do. That is to say, it meets the requirements. But it is also a great way to make sure that it does *not* do something that it is not supposed to, or that the execution fails. Basically, it is a way for developers to quality-assure their own code.

There are basically three different types of automated testing, when it comes to your code:

- *Unit testing* investigates the way that a function works, separate from any other interference. This is very useful for complex functions, like encryption services for example, when you know exactly for each input what type of output will match it.

  However, using it too much can easily bring things to a point where you have a large number of tests that don't necessarily test for anything.

- *Integration testing* is used to check how various systems interact with each other. One example is the integration between your system and an external payment system. It is not difficult to imagine why you would want to make sure that a code change that you are pushing does not break the payment processing system.

- *End-to-end (system) testing* is used to test the entire application, starting with the frontend. When you are developing an application, you normally have two or three separate systems, such as a Development environment, a Staging environment for your final checks, and a Production application. Using system testing enables you to directly plug into the frontend of your application and use the system exactly like any other of your users would. This approach has the advantage that it is the most-encompassing method of testing, meaning that most of the code and the integration will be checked with a single test. Therefore, end-to-end testing is also one of the most commonly used types of testing.

Such end-to-end testing systems also offer you the possibility to take screenshots or even small videos of your tests, so you can also manually check them, if needed. They can emulate virtually any browser, test mobile application, and much more.

Two of the most commonly used such testing systems is Selenium for Java and Playwright for JavaScript. This book uses Playwright. You can take a look at `https://playwright.dev/` for a better understanding of how this works and what it is capable to do.

How the testing should be done, and which parts should be tested, is a matter of debate. Some companies believe in minimal testing, and others test every piece of code. Some teams even rely on triggers in their pipeline that block merge requests if the code does not have at least 80 percent automated testing.

My personal opinion is that you should write as much end-to-end testing as possible, as it has the following advantages:

1. It will test all of your code and system in one go, whether it is backend, frontend, infrastructure, or anything else.

2. It tests things in exactly the same way that the users interact with your systems.

In contrast to writing unit tests or integration tests, this approach has the following advantages:

1. They are easy to write. Compared to an end-to-end test, you have a lot more control over what exactly should happen, in different cases.

2. They are more reliable. Because they usually run in isolation, they run very fast, and produce a relatively small amount of false positives. That means if you see your test in the red, there is a good chance that you broke something

In short, testing is there to give you confidence that your code will not break anything important. It is necessary that you find a balance between the different types of testing and your actual development work.

That being said, the next section looks at the different types of tests, explains how they work, and covers how can you write tests for your application.

Unit Testing

As described, unit tests are built to verify that a certain unit of your code works the way it was designed, regardless of its context. Unit testing is mostly used to check the functionality of methods, functions, and small components.

Imagine that you have just built the following function that you badly need inside of your codebase. It is a very simple function, one that simply adds two numbers, but it is enough to illustrate the testing process:

```
const addNumbers = (a, b) => {
  return a + b;
};

module.exports = { addNumbers };
```

Now add this function inside a file in the frontend folder, for example a file named numberHelper.js. Why should you save this file in the frontend folder? First of all, you will build unit tests around code that already exists. So they have to be inside of the frontend or the backend folder. As a result, the frontend folder will do just fine, for this example.

In order to start testing, you need to install the testing framework, called jest (https://jestjs.io/). Just run the npm install jest command. Then, open package.js and add the following code to it:

```
"scripts": {
  "start": "react-scripts start",
  "build": "react-scripts build",
  "test": "react-scripts test",
  "eject": "react-scripts eject",
  "jstest": "jest"
},
```

Now you can run your scripts by typing npm run jstest.

In order to start writing tests, create a folder called tests, and there, create a file called helperTests.test.js. Note the extension test.js. That way, the test framework knows where all the tests are located and can run them all at once.

Now write your first test as follows:

```
const numberHelper = require("../src/numberHelper");

describe("numberHelper unit test group", () => {
  it("should add two numbers correctly", () => {
    expect(numberHelper.addNumbers(2, 2)).toBe(4);
  });
});
```

If you run this command, you will see that the test runs green:

```
C:\Users\Radu\CRM\13.3\frontend>npm run jstest

> frontend@0.1.0 jstest
> jest

Browserslist: caniuse-lite is outdated. Please run:
  npx browserslist@latest --update-db
  Why you should do it regularly: https://github.com/browserslist/browserslist#browsers-data-updating
 PASS  tests/helperTests.test.js
  numberHelper unit test group
    √ should add two numbers correctly (2 ms)

Test Suites: 1 passed, 1 total
Tests:       1 passed, 1 total
Snapshots:   0 total
Time:        0.424 s, estimated 1 s
Ran all test suites.
```

Let's take a look at what exactly the code is doing. The describe part is there to add order to the tests. It basically means that this is just a collection of tests, and they check inside of the code whatever you summarized in the description. Then, the it part is the start of a single test.

Seeing how you just tested what is supposed to go right with your code, now you'll see how you can test what is supposed to go wrong. This is also an important part of testing.

For example, you know that you cannot call your functions with fewer or more parameters. So you can test that:

```
it("throws errors when parameters are not correct", () => {
  expect(numberHelper.addNumbers()).toBe(NaN);
});
```

This test case will also make your code check green.

As you can see, there are numerous things that you can test about a single function. You need to find a balance though, which is where your role as a developer comes in. You need to find a good spot between testing what you want to test, or have to test, but also not overburden the application with too many tests. Every time you change the function, you also have to change the tests.

Test Driven Development

Test Drive Development (or TDD) is a concept that many organizations have implemented, and can be summarized as the type of development where, before you start writing your code, you write a relevant test. After the test is written, you see what fails, you fix it by writing new lines of code, until it is green, and then you refactor the code. This is how the mantra became "red ➤ green ➤ refactor".

Consider a function that you just wrote. Imagine that the team that uses this function asks you to make sure that if only one parameter is provided, instead of both, an error is thrown. As a result, you remove your last test and write a new one. This makes the test now look like this:

```javascript
const numberHelper = require("../src/numberHelper");

describe("numberHelper unit test group", () => {
  it("should add two numbers correctly", () => {
    expect(numberHelper.addNumbers(2, 2)).toBe(4);
  });

  it("throws errors when parameters are not correct", () => {
    expect(() => numberHelper.addNumbers()).toThrow(
      "Please provide two parameters"
    );
    expect(() => numberHelper.addNumbers(2)).toThrow(
      "Please provide two parameters"
    );
  });
});
```

If you run the tests, you now get an error. That means you are at the red step:

You need to make the tests run green. In order to do that, go into the function and determine whether the parameters provided were correct. If they were not correct, throw an error:

```
const addNumbers = (a, b) => {
  if (a === undefined || b === undefined) {
    throw new Error("Please provide two parameters");
  }

  return a + b;
};
```

And now, your test will run green again:

```
C:\Users\Radu\CRM\13.3\frontend>npm run jstest

> frontend@0.1.0 jstest
> jest

Browserslist: caniuse-lite is outdated. Please run:
  npx browserslist@latest --update-db
  Why you should do it regularly: https://github.com/browserslist/browserslist#browsers-data-updating
 PASS  tests/helperTests.test.js
  numberHelper unit test group
    ✓ should add two numbers correctly (2 ms)
    ✓ throws errors when parameters are not correct (7 ms)

Test Suites: 1 passed, 1 total
Tests:       2 passed, 2 total
Snapshots:   0 total
Time:        0.464 s, estimated 1 s
Ran all test suites.
```

You can skip the refactor stage, since your code is well written from the start. But this would be where you bring the code up to standard, if that is not the case.

Now run this test again. Say that the other team had an issue, where the function was called with two parameters, but as strings, and that led to an error. You now have a new requirement—when the function receives two parameters but they are not numbers, it should throw an error and ask for numbers.

Here is the new test that takes care of that situation:

```
expect(() => numberHelper.addNumbers("par1", "par2")).toThrow(
    "Please provide numbers"
);
```

```
Test Suites: 1 failed, 1 total
Tests:       1 failed, 1 passed, 2 total
Snapshots:   0 total
Time:        0.557 s, estimated 1 s
Ran all test suites.
```

This function takes care of such an event, where both parameters are strings, so that the tests run green.

```
if (typeof a !== "number" || typeof b !== "number") {
  throw new Error("Please provide numbers");
}
```

```
PASS  tests/helperTests.test.js
  numberHelper unit test group
    ✓ should add two numbers correctly (2 ms)
    ✓ throws errors when parameters are not correct (7 ms)

Test Suites: 1 passed, 1 total
Tests:       2 passed, 2 total
Snapshots:   0 total
Time:        0.436 s, estimated 1 s
Ran all test suites.
```

And that is it! That is how you do test driven development (TDD).
There is, of course, a lot of controversy about whether this should actually
be done in the first place, or whether tests should be written at the end
of the coding session, once you actually know what you need to test.
The advantage of TDD is that you can always guarantee, with tests, that
your code works as it should. It also forces you to figure out early in the
development if all of the requirements have been completely understood.
The downside is that development takes longer, you end up with a large
number of tests that you have to maintain every time you change your
code, and it is difficult to implement when the feature requires a large
amount of interaction between the frontend and the backend. I personally
only use TDD when I need to build complex, singular functions.

Integration Tests

Suppose that your function is now so well tested that you are fully
confident that it will work as intended. However, your app has multiple
such functions, which continuously interact with each other. Because of
that, in order to have full confidence in your systems, it makes sense to
look into more complex test cases.

This is exactly where integration testing comes in. It offers you the
ability to verify how two or more functions interact with each other.

To understand this, you'll build a new function that uses the previous
one. It should be something simple, so that you can write some tests for it.
You can make it more complicated later. To start, build something this:

```
const totalNumber = () => {
  const total = addNumbers(5, 10);

  return 'Our Total Number is ${total}';
};
```

Now, write a small test for it:

```
describe("integration test for totalNumber", () => {
  it("should return the correct string", () => {
    expect(numberHelper.totalNumber()).toBe("Our Total Number
    is 15");
  });
});
```

This may not look very impressive at the moment, but you just wrote your first integration test! That is because you are simultaneously testing the `totalNumber()` function and the way that it interacts with the `addNumbers()` function.

Now you can build something more complicated. Assume that the `totalNumber()` function is supposed to deliver the total number of customers. It does this by calling two APIs and formatting the result. Something along the lines of this:

```
const totalNumber = () => {
  const amazonClients = apiCalls.amazonTotalClients();
  const ebayClients = apiCalls.ebayTotalClients();
  const total = addNumbers(amazonClients, ebayClients);

  return 'Our Total Number is ${total}';
};
```

This function will first call the API of Amazon (or pretend to, at least, for the sake of the demonstration) to retrieve a number of clients. It will then call the eBay API and collect the customers that you have there. It will then call the initial function, `addNumbers()`, using the new data that it collected.

Since you cannot accept that the actual API calls will happen every time your tests run—because either they will be slow or you will have to pay additionally for the API calls—it is better to somehow mock the data coming back, when testing the function.

For this purpose, you can create APIs that will pretend to return the data from the third-party websites. Create a new file called apiCalls.js and add the following code to it:

```
// for simplicity, we will pretend these are their own modules
const amazonTotalClients = () => 52;
const ebayTotalClients = () => 12;

module.exports = {
  amazonTotalClients,
  ebayTotalClients,
};
```

But now there is a dilemma. How exactly can you test such a function, if you do not know how the APIs are going to behave? And besides that, it is not really your job to be testing third-party APIs in the first place. You therefore need to mock the APIs. Basically, you tell the jest framework that you will pretend that you know what type of data will be returned by the two APIs, and that way, you can continue with your tests.

```
const numberHelper = require("../src/numberHelper");
const apiCalls = require("../src/apiCalls");

jest.mock("../src/apiCalls");

describe("integration test for totalNumber", () => {
  it("should return the correct string", () => {
    apiCalls.amazonTotalClients.mockReturnValue(12);
    apiCalls.ebayTotalClients.mockReturnValue(13);
```

```
  expect(numberHelper.totalNumber()).toBe("Our Total Number
  is 25");
});
});
```

You can see that the API calls were mocked by the test. When running the integration tests, the testing framework will pretend that each API call will return the numbers 12 and 13, and never actually call the API on the third-party side. As a result, your total number is 25 instead of the actual 64 that would be returned if you were to actually call it.

I use this mocking property pretty often, because it allows me to test parts of my code, without access to the database or to a third-party API. This is especially helpful when you are trying to create new users or are testing payment systems. In such cases, you would not want your tests to be performed against production data. As a result, you can mock such calls, so that you can test your integration services in isolation to the systems that you normally plug into.

One of the best ways to use integration testing is to do GraphQL testing. That is, you emulate your database and/or API calls, and then access your backend application via the GraphQL interface. That way, you can test your entire backend segment in isolation. Doing this type of testing is, in my view, one of the best ways to perform integration testing.

End-to-End Testing

So far, you have investigated the process of testing your entire system. Your tests plug directly into your functions and check various points inside of them. However, your end users will not be accessing your functions directly, but will interact with them using your trusted user interface. Hence the name of end-to-end testing—from the user to the database.

As a result, you must test your application just as if you were an actual user. That is, you need to open a browser and access your application. It would also be nice to test various browsers to make sure that all users will be able to access your system as you intended.

There are two big libraries that can achieve this using JavaScript: Cypress (`www.cypress.io`) and Playwright (`https://playwright. dev/`). This chapter uses Playwright, but they are very similar and use similar syntax.

The first step is to install the library. Do this inside a new folder called `tests`. Then run the following command:

```
npm init playwright@latest
```

After this, make sure that your frontend and backend are both running. Then open a browser and verify that you can access the system (see Figure 8-1). If you cannot access it, Playwright can't either.

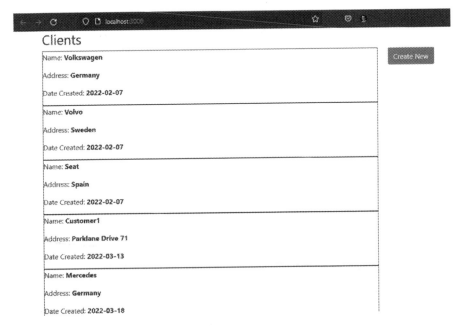

Figure 8-1. *The application is running*

Now that the application is running, it's time to determine what exactly you are trying to test at the moment—the user path for the test case. I propose that your tests try to create a new customer, just like a user would do:

1. Enter the URL of the application and verify that there is actually a web page being displayed, and that the Create New button is displayed.

2. Click the Create New button and fill in the form.

3. Save your efforts. Verify that no error is shown.

4. Test that your new customer is displayed.

Now you'll see exactly how to do this in the Playwright environment. First go to the tests folder, where you installed Playwright, and find the folder called tests inside of it (I know that it is a bit confusing). In that folder, there is a file. Just delete that file, as it is an empty example. Create a new file called customerTest.spec.js. Note that the extension .spec.js is used so that Playwright knows which files should be run.

```
import { test, expect } from "@playwright/test";

const URL = "http://localhost:3000/";
test("Page is Loading and displaying", async ({ page }) => {
  await page.goto(URL);
  await page.waitForSelector("text=Create New");
  await expect(page).toHaveTitle("React App");
  await expect(page.locator("text=Create New")).toBeVisible();
});
```

Note the await keyword in this code. All of the functions that have to do with the browser are asynchronous, that is, they will not render a result immediately, but will come back once the result has been produced.

You basically just go to the URL and wait for the button to appear. Once that the button is there, you check that the page has a title, and that the button is being rendered.

Now, for the second part, creating a client. It would be nice for your popup form to have some classes or IDs, so that you can test them. Go to the ./frontend/createCustomer.js file and add some classes to it:

```
<Modal.Body>
  Name
  <Form.Control
    value={customerName}
    className="customerName"
    onChange={(e) => setCustomerName(e.target.value)}
    // e is here an event, so we get the value of the
    change event
  />
  Address
  <Form.Control
    value={customerAddress}
    className="customerAddress"
    onChange={(e) => setCustomerAddress(e.target.value)}
  />
</Modal.Body>
```

You can see your changes by inspecting one of the inputs inside of the popup. Just right-click and then choose Inspect (see Figure 8-2).

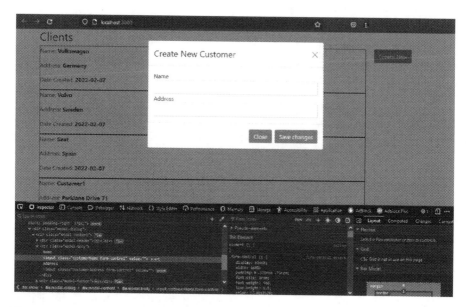

Figure 8-2. *Inspecting the popup elements to see your new classes*

With those classes, you can build the rest of your code. You can then run it, and it will test your app in all three of the major browsers: Mozilla, Chrome (this includes Edge), and Safari.

```
import { test, expect } from "@playwright/test";

const URL = "http://localhost:3000/";
test("Page is Loading and displaying", async ({ page }) => {
  await page.goto(URL);
  await page.waitForSelector("text=Create New");
  await expect(page).toHaveTitle("React App");
  await expect(page.locator("text=Create New")).toBeVisible();

  // click on the button
  await page.click("text=Create New");
  await page.waitForSelector(".customerName");
```

```
const testCustomer = "Test-Cusomer";
const testAddress = "test Address";
await page.fill(".customerName", testCustomer);
await page.fill(".customerAddress", testAddress);
await page.click(".modal-footer .btn-primary"); //Save data

//See that the data was saved
await page.waitForSelector("text=" + testCustomer);
await expect(page.locator("text=" + testCustomer)).
toBeVisible();
await expect(page.locator("text=" + testAddress)).
toBeVisible();
});
```

Note that because you use the customer name and address at least two times, it is now a constant. That ensures that your code does not repeat too much.

If you run your tests (by running the `npx playwright test` command), you will instantly get a green light:

If you add `headless: false` inside of the use block in the config file, the browser will open and automatically follow along with your test case. That is also where you set up how many types of browsers you want to run in your tests. I usually only have one, and that is Chrome.

Homework

Try writing your own tests:

1. Follow the instructions of this chapter to create at least one unit test and one end-to-end test.

2. If you have interesting ideas, extend the end-to-end test.

Summary

Testing is an integral part of development. It is a lot more important when you have a complex application. Testing gives developers the confidence that the things that they deploy do not break important functionalities in the existing system.

Finding a balance between development and testing is always difficult, so as a beginner, it is a good idea to start with the 80/20 rule. That is, spend 80 percent of your time on development, and 20 percent on testing. Depending on your industry, this could be vastly different. For example, a bank would have many more tests built into their code than a startup that has a presentation website or created a small demo for their client. But this is the job of the developer—to find the correct balance.

CHAPTER 9

Other Frameworks and Technologies

You do not need to build every functionality in your application. It is actually quite the contrary! Most of the time, the best answer is to look for ready-made solutions on the market. Some of them cost a bit of money, but can be worth it, but in most cases, the ready-made solutions are free.

This chapter goes through a few examples of things that you should know about, if you are to become a programmer. Some are simply concepts that you should be familiar with, while others are exactly these premade solutions that might come in handy in your projects.

Creating a Login System

A proper login system is the cornerstone of any web application. It serves two important, maybe even fundamental, purposes of your application.

On the one hand, it allows you to know who is viewing the current page. That way, you can display only data that is relevant to that user, such as their messages, friend posts, private files, and so on. Basically, it provides you with user context.

Another fundamental part of a login system is not allowing other people to break into a user's private sphere. That is, making sure that only the proper user has access to the data that they should have access to. Them, and nobody else.

The next section looks at what it takes to make such a system work.

© Radu Nicoara 2023
R. Nicoara, *How to be a Web Developer*, https://doi.org/10.1007/978-1-4842-9663-9_9

Login Systems

Almost all applications need a login system. However, seeing how this is the fundamental building block of the applications' security, it is not necessarily a good idea to build it from scratch.

Besides the fact that you would then need to deal with the hassle of fixing potential bugs or deal with every possible type of attack, it would also be an extremely difficult challenge, because you have to integrate the login process with all of the possible vendors, such as Google, Facebook, LinkedIn, and so on.

For actual application that you would build for production, I highly recommend using a library that has everything prebuilt, where you would only need to call a certain function.

One of the most commonly used libraries is PassportJS, found at www.passportjs.org/. It is very flexible and most certainly offers you all that you need for your login system.

That being said, let's consider how you would start building a login system, if you had to.

Any website that needs a login system is basically split into two parts:

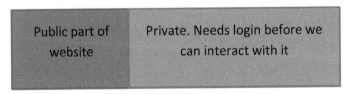

1. The *public* part includes the landing page, the contact page, the terms and conditions, and so on.

2. The *private* part includes sensitive data and will most likely take up most of your website.

The frontend part can be easily split into these two parts by just checking the user data before the render. The way you can tell if somebody is logged in is by using *cookies*.

Cookies

A *cookie* is a variable that is stored inside of a person's browser that contains personal information about the person, such as their login credentials. It can have an expiration date, which is usually set to 30 days. This is the way you can follow a person around the Internet.

There is however a restriction, which is that a website cannot read the cookies from another website. This is a built-in security feature for all modern browsers. You would not want a website that you visit to have access to your login data from a different website.

```
document.cookie = "username=John Doe"; //we set a cookie

let x = document.cookie;
// will return all cookies in one string: cookie1=value;
cookie2=value; cookie3=value;
```

This way, when a user comes back to your website a few days later, they can skip the login part, because the site remembers who they are.

For the private part of the website, the one that needs authentication, the program first checks if the user has the proper cookies. If they do not, it redirects them to the landing page. This can easily be done in the frontend, using the index.js file:

```
<ApolloProvider client={client}>
  {isUserLoggedIn() ? <App /> : <LandingPage />}
</ApolloProvider>
```

If the user is not logged in, the program does not render the app, but instead shows the landing page, which will contain the login screen.

An additional safety measure is that the backend also needs to check this authentication before it returns any data.

MD5

Here are the login steps for users to access your website:

1. The user creates an account using a username and password.

2. Your program stores the login data in your database.

3. The user tries to log in using the previously-provided username and password.

4. You check the data provided against the data in the database. If they match, the program provides the user with a cookie.

However, it would be an incredibly bad idea to store the password in clear text inside of the database. Just imagine what would happen if somebody, somehow, got access to your database. It would look like the following:

id	username	password	email
1	bestUser123	StrongPass123&	bestUser123@cool.com
2	star_user_2000	BestStrongPass@5	star_user_2000@mega-star.xyz

The main problem that you can see here is that people usually have the same password on many other websites, so that means that breaking into one could possibly mean breaking into them all.

That is why it is useful to have a function that takes text as input, such as a password, does some processing, and returns as a one-way output some random text that cannot be deciphered. This is called a *hash* function, and one of the most common ones is *MD5*.

Note   Keep in mind that MD5 is an outdated algorithm, and currently it is recommended that you use a better algorithm like SHA-2. However, for this exercise, and some other less secure features, MD5 will do just fine.

MD5 will take your passwords and encrypt them, so that you only need to store the encrypted versions in the database and encrypt the password provided by the user before checking it into the database.

- StrongPass123& → **5e7afa1d53835a8e88a98aefb 89b64f4**

- BestStrongPass@5 → **64d6f8cad75daf9a891dc575af 061bd7**

A hash will always return the same output for the same input. Another feature of the hash is that if you change the input just a little bit, the output fundamentally changes, making it basically impossible to trace the original string.

Coming back to your app, if you only have the hash in the database, you can rehash the user-provided password and check the hash against the one that you have inside the database.

Since there is no way to get the original string back, and the encryption will always return the same key for the same input string, a database leak will not cause too many issues. Using hashes, your database now looks like this, so there is not a big security risk associated with it:

id	username	password	email
1	bestUser123	5e7afa1d53835a8e88a98aefb89b64f4	bestUser123@cool.com
2	star_user_2000	64d6f8cad75daf9a891dc575af061bd7	star_user_2000@mega-star.xyz

Other Technologies You Should Know About

This section briefly covers some other technologies that you will probably use in your career as a programmer. I do not go in depth into any of them, but there are links where you can find more info.

Open Source

A big part of the technologies that you will use as a developer is considered open source. That means, first of all, that the source code of the software is open to the public, so that everyone who wants to look at the code can do so. This also means that the chances of there being security issues in the code are minimal, since there is a large number of developers looking over things.

Another big advantage of open source projects is that, generally speaking, it does not cost anything to use them. Although some have premium products on offer, such as better support or certain extensions, it does not cost anything for you as a developer to create your own software using open source technologies, and then use the solution. This is in contrast to some other commercial solutions, which request that you pay a part of your proceedings to them for using their software in your builds.

The most important part of using open source is that everybody can add to it. That means that if you ever find a bug, you are absolutely encouraged to try to fix it. It also means that there is a way for you to try out your skills, if you so desire.

Famous open source projects include the following:

- GIMP, an image editing program

- VLC Media Player, a video player

- WordPress, a content management system

- TensorFlow, a machine learning library in Python

- Linux, an operating system

- LibreOffice, a free alternative to Microsoft Office

GIT

Git is one of the most commonly used technologies inside of the programming space. It is a versioning control tool that enables you to practically make a copy of the current code structure. With this copy, you can change things around as much as you want without affecting the main code.

Once you are done with the code, you can simply merge your changes back into the main branch (see Figure 9-1).

Figure 9-1. *Structure of the Git branches*

The big advantage of using Git technology for development is that:

- The main code remains unchanged while you develop

- You can always revert to a previous commit if you encounter any issues.

- There is a history of who did what, where.

- Merge requests can be reviewed individually, before they are merged back into the live code.

- You can attach triggers to the merging, so that once a merge is completed, the new code can be pushed to production, for example.

If you want to find out more, go to `https://github.com` and create a free account. Then you can have your own repository where you can play around. You can also use this repository to build a small portfolio to share with potential recruiters.

You will get a more in-depth discussion about the Git technology in a later chapter of this book.

Azure/Amazon Cloud Providers

Now that your app is in development, you have to think about what exactly to do with it once you are finished and want your users to use it.

You can use any number of hosting providers for this purpose, but using one of the big names in the industry, such as Amazon Web Services (AWS) or Microsoft Azure, has some very specific advantages:

- A separate database layer that can scale up and down with your application.

- Specific libraries for your users to log into, which the vendor will take care of. You just have to call a function inside of your app.

- Scalable file and data storage, if you need to build, for example, a social media platform.

- Docker support (see Chapter 10).

- Possibility to integrate multiple applications, using the provided APIs.

Both offer a free version, so if you want to learn more, you can simply open an account and start looking around.

Docker

Docker enables you to create containers for your applications. But what exactly is a *container*?

Imagine that you have just finished developing your application, and you now want to deploy it to production, so that your users have access to it. The normal way would be to create a server somewhere like Amazon or Azure, and set up your app there. This would include the backend, the frontend, the database, all the libraries, all the setups, ports, libraries, and so on.

The issue with this is that if the server updates the operating system, or you need to change the vendor, you have to start from scratch and perform the setup all over again.

It is exactly for this case that Docker was built. You can set up an image and detail exactly which operating system it should use, which ports go where, and which servers start up with which files inside of them. It will all just turn on and work in any machine that you try to run it from.

Say you create an app in a Docker image and send the entire package to your friend, who uses a different operating system. All they would have to do is to start up the Docker image, and everything would simply just work.

NoSQL

mongoDB

Just as is generally the case, data that you have to save in the database is normally thought of in a structured manner, and as a result, you can always save it inside a predefined table and access it based on the columns of those tables.

However, you may stumble into a case where you need to save and later retrieve data that is not structured. Think about logs or collections of data points from various machines.

You could always just save this data as text and later pull and parse it, so you get your arrays and objects back, but you would lose the ability to query the data.

For this reason, you could instead choose a NoSQL database, such as MongoDB. NoSQL databases enable you to have flexible schema, so that you can easily save and query data with any structure. The same idea applies to DynamoDB, the NoSQL database from Amazon.

However, NoSQL databases are generally a niche product, and they are rarely encountered in day-to-day life.

If you want to find out more, visit their websites at `www.mongodb.com/` and `https://aws.amazon.com/dynamodb`.

JIRA

Jira is one of the most commonly used applications for managing development projects and the work that teams need to perform. It helps teams plan, track, report, and assign their work. It also helps teams with various Agile methodologies.

Jira helps with the backlog of tickets, with sprint planning, and even has some automation behind it. But before everything else, Jira is a ticket management system (see Figure 9-2).

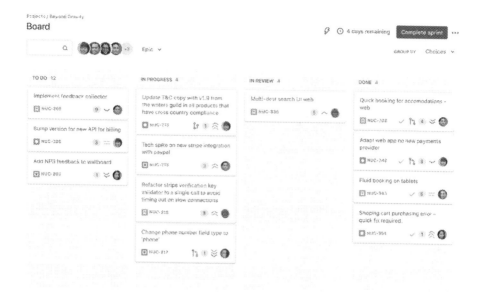

Figure 9-2. Screenshot of a Jira board

You can discover more, and even see a demo of Jira, by visiting their official website at `www.jira.com`.

You will learn a lot more about this tool in a future chapter, but at the moment, it is sufficient to say that working on a software development team is a lot more efficient when you're using a tool like Jira.

WordPress

WordPress is a content management system (CMS) and one of the easiest and most powerful ways to create almost any website. It initially began as a blogging platform, but it quickly evolved into much more than that. WordPress currently offers solutions ranging from blogging and static presentation websites, to online shopping platforms. It gives you the advantage of installing and maintaining a website without any coding knowledge.

WordPress is probably the most commonly used solution for any website that is simple enough to only contain a static set of pages, but it also has extensions for anything from sending emails to e-commerce. It allows users to easily install new themes for the website, edit text, create and link new pages, and everything else that an average owner of a small-to-medium website could want. Login integrations and payment methods can also be added to the website with just a few clicks.

Being one of the most commonly used platforms on the Internet has additional advantages. Finding free stuff for your WordPress website is not difficult at all, and any issues you might stumble on are easy to investigate and fix (see Figure 9-3).

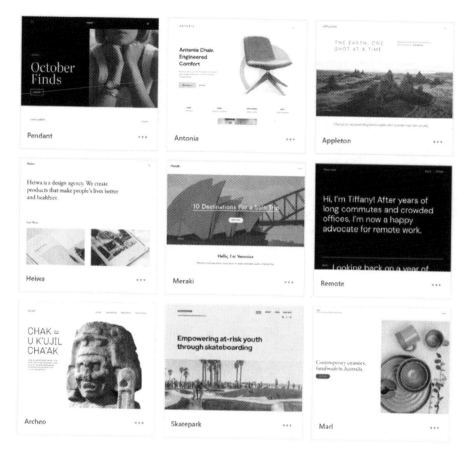

Figure 9-3. *A sample collection of free themes offered by WordPress*

The most important part of being a developer is not being afraid of using prebuilt solutions. There is no use in reinventing the wheel. So, feel free to use WordPress or Squarespace for a client who needs a blog or a presentation website, and Shopify or Adobe Commerce for a client who needs an e-commerce solution.

Summary

One of the characteristics of any good engineer is knowing where to channel the effort, in order to maximize the desired outcome. This primarily translates into knowing which technologies exist on the market and knowing how to use them.

Unfortunately, this chapter only covered a small amount of everything that the Internet has to offer, in terms of efficient ways of working. As a result, it is up to you to keep up to speed with the current state of affairs and the current trends in your domain.

PART III

Landing Your First Role

CHAPTER 10

Your First Job

After you have gathered enough information about web development, it is time to search for your first job. How exactly do you reach that point? What steps can you take to improve your chances of getting a job, and therefore, start your career in the IT industry?

The first important point to keep in mind is that you will be looking for a junior position. That means that if you already have some experience in a certain domain, you need to be prepared to take a step backward for a few years. You are at the beginning of a very good career path, but you are also starting from scratch.

One of the best ways to transition into IT is to apply to jobs with fewer requirements, such as the ones at startups. The downside is that for a year or two, while you become good at programming, you will most likely not be paid as well. On the other hand, the experience that you gain is going to make up for the sacrifice in the long run. I have personally been through this process, and most of my friends who work in IT have been through this as well.

An internship is also a good way to go, but make sure that it is a paid one. Even after a few weeks of working as a developer, you will bring value to the team. Don't sell yourself short and don't get scammed.

All of these factors, of course, depend on your country and your geographical region, as well as the general economic conditions. With that in mind, ask your peers for advice. You can find out more about how to do this in the "Networking and Volunteering" section of this chapter.

© Radu Nicoara 2023
R. Nicoara, *How to be a Web Developer*, https://doi.org/10.1007/978-1-4842-9663-9_10

Creating a Portfolio

One of the best things you can do is develop your skills further. In addition to that, you need to prove your skills to a potential employer. As a result, it is a very good idea to start a personal project or to continue the CRM that you started to build in this book.

The first step is to head over to https://github.com/. Create a free account there, and then install the Git software on your computer. After this, push your code into a Git repository, so that you can easily share it with potential recruiters.

Then, think about something that you enjoy and create a small presentation website. It does not have to be hosted anywhere. Just get more familiar with all the things that web development has to offer.

Ask your friends if any of them need a website for anything. This way you are also helping a friend out and adding projects to your portfolio.

Just as a personal anecdote, I used to love reading the travel blog that two of my friends created. It was not working properly on mobile, and this was my main way of catching up with them. As a result, I offered to fix their website for free. Luckily, it was a WordPress website, so it was all finished in a few days. By doing this, I got to spend time with my friends, help them out, and contribute to a nice project that I was using.

Networking and Volunteering

An important part of any career revolves around the people you know. And the IT industry is no different in this respect. It helps you a lot if you are involved in a local or online community. Consider the following ways to network.

Go to meetups, if you live around a big metropolitan area. Big cities usually have a big IT community, and this enables you to meet other peers. Where I live, for example, in Berlin, Germany, there are multiple IT communities, including a local React community, a Women Who Code, a Tech Enthusiasts meetup, and so on. All of these can be found if you go to meetup.com.

Find online or open projects. This really depends what you are good at and what you like to do, but there are a large number of open-source projects in all kinds of domains, from pharmaceutical to videogames. If you can think of something that you personally have an interest in, you can look for how to help.

Another favorite of mine is to *go to hackathons.* You don't need to be a specialist in anything. Just go there and have fun. Hackathons have various themes, and not all of them are highly technical. I once won a hackathon with a WordPress website and a small customizable Android app. Not because my solution was the most advanced, but because the NGO that the Hackathon was trying to help needed a sustainable solution that they could operate. So you don't need to build complex solutions in order to have an impact. On the contrary, sometimes simpler answers are the best.

Consider *rebuilding the website of local associations.* As mentioned, I sometimes do this as well, even to this day. This type of project can test your technical skills a bit, as well as deliver something to your community. Look for associations and NGOs that look like they could use a website upgrade and get in contact with them. Most will be highly appreciative of such an offer.

Join online communities, such as Reddit. There, you can find a very and large choice of online content and discussions. Check out /r/ITCareerQuestions/, /r/Web_Development/, and /r/react/. My favorite is /r/ProgrammerHumor/, just because I like a good laugh from time to time.

Go to stackoverflow.com and look at the various questions and answers there. It is, indeed, less of a community, but sometimes, it can be quite entertaining.

Freelancing

An excellent way to gather experience is to start doing some freelancing jobs. This comes with the added benefit of providing some small amount of additional income. All you need to do to start along this path is head either to `www.upwork.com/` or to `www.freelancer.com/` and open an account.

At the beginning of my career, when I was not earning as much, I was almost doubling my income with weekend projects that I got through freelancing. Some of my friends have quit their jobs entirely and now only work as freelancers.

Since you are starting a new career, I advise that you look for jobs that match your knowledge, and be open and transparent to a potential customer about the fact that you are still learning and looking for experience. An easy way to get started is to take some side jobs for free, so that you start having a reputation within the community. Most people will not refuse a free job, so just make sure to take something that is relatively small.

Once you have a few clients, they keep coming back. For me, for example, after about six months on the platform, I was no longer looking for new projects, as I had three customers who gave me enough work to fill my free time. Sometimes even more.

All things considered, it is a good idea to look into this line of work, especially at the beginning. You will have lots of flexibility, and will absolutely learn a lot, including soft skills.

Writing a Good Resume

Your resume is your window to the professional world. It is important that it's well done. One way to achieve this is to use a template. Do not be afraid to do that. I also use a template that I have adjusted to my needs.

Make sure to list all of your experience, in reverse chronological order, with bullets points for your main responsibilities in each job.

Have a separate section for volunteer work and a separate part dedicated to programming languages that you know. An interesting trend that I have seen is people rating their knowledge on a scale from 1 to 5, similar to what you see in Figure 10-1.

React   **SQL**   **Python**
●●●○○   ●●●●○   ●●●○○

Figure 10-1. *Skill rating system in a resume*

Don't forget to cover soft skills, as this is a very important part of any hiring. A manager is not only looking to hire an engineer, but also an actual human being. They would much rather hire someone who is average technically but can work great on a team, rather than a rock-star developer who can only work alone, and is half the time in a bad mood. Therefore, focus on how you work with others and what makes you a good hire from that perspective.

One way to set yourself apart is to have a letter of intent. Just write a few paragraphs about who you are and what motivates you. Explain what you are looking for in the job that the company is posting, and what your plans are if they hire you.

As always, it is important to know how to sell yourself. Try to make it easy for the person reading your information to understand what makes you a good fit, what your strong skills are, and what would make you a good addition to their team.

Finding and Applying for a Job

All being said, I recommend that you browse the job listings in your area, so you get accustomed to the state of the market and see what types of skills and technologies are in demand. This will also give you a general direction on where you need to develop further, what technologies are currently of interest in the market, and even broad salary expectations.

The best place to look for jobs are on regional or national job posting portals. It makes sense to go where the companies are posting as well. Every country, and even every state, has websites specific to them, where companies list their jobs. Use your favorite search engine to find out more.

Another good place to look is the job section of LinkedIn. Most companies also post on LinkedIn, so it is a good aggregator. Look for keywords like "Software Developer," "JavaScript," "React," "Fullstack Developer," "Web Developer," and so on.

Remember that you don't need to meet every single requirement on a posted position. If you meet more than half of the requirements, you have a shot at that job. Even if you don't meet them all, you still have a chance to convince the company that you are a fast learner, and that they should give you an opportunity to prove your worth.

Most positions are not posted by the people actually working the job, who know what exactly is it that one would absolutely need for the job. They are often posted by the managing leads or the HR department. As a result, they are describing the ideal candidate, with even sometimes the hope that they can convince a senior engineer to come work for a junior position. That is how you end up seeing entry positions that require three years of React experience, for example.

Just as a side note, generally every two-three years, you should step up in your position. If that does not happen at your current company, then it should at a new one. After three years, a junior programmer normally becomes a mid-developer, because they can work semi-autonomously.

And a mid-developer, after another three years or so, becomes a senior developer. That is the stage where they start to mentor others, lead projects and integrations, and so on.

Take a look at some examples of the requirements that are most commonly posted:

- *Completed studies in a technical field* is one of the most common requirements. It will be just a minor disadvantage if you have completed studies in a non-technical field, and if you explain in your letter of intent that you plan to switch, and that you are highly motivated and hard working. But having no studies is seen as a general disadvantage and can only be compensated by years of experience.

- *Knowledge of Scrum methodologies* is another requirement that you often see in job postings. Luckily, I cover this topic in the next chapter.

- *Knowledge of API concepts and software development principles.* This is the main focus of this book. To offer you an oversight into how software development is being done, and what an API should look like. In this case, that is using GraphQL. Another way this is phrased is as having basic knowledge of IT architecture, Software development, and databases. As long as you continue to develop your skills in this domain, you should be covered.

- *Being a team player, or other soft skills, such as presentation skills, communication, and so on.* As mentioned, being able to work on a team, being flexible, open, and communicative is an advantage in the IT industry. A good manager will pick a decent

179

> developer who works great on a team over a great
> developer who is unpleasant to be around any day of
> the week. No one person is worth an entire team, no
> matter how good they are.

Of course, some things are implicitly requested, such as motivation to learn and interest in web development. But since you picked up this book, it is safe to assume that you do not lack in any of these areas.

In your letter of intent, you should try to address every item in the requirement that you even remotely fulfill. This will give you the highest probability of being selected for an interview.

Think about the size of the companies that you apply to as well. It makes to have realistic expectations about what awaits you in each case. Keep in mind that the following are gross generalizations, so take everything I say with a grain of salt.

With startups, or small companies, funding is usually tight. That means that they ideally want to hire experts for salaries of juniors or mids. One way they try to bridge the gap is by providing employees with equity. Those shares in the company, may (or most likely may not) be worth something in the future, keeping in mind that statistically, 90 percent of all startups fail in the first five years. In addition to this, working at a startup usually mean a high work load and lots of overtime. It is just the nature of the business. You might also be asked to do things that are not necessarily in your area of work, from server maintenance, to cleaning the kitchen. It depends on the company. However, there are also advantages to working for small companies. You might find it easier to find a job at a startup, as there aren't as many people competing for such positions. Another advantage is that your work will be visible. You will work closer to the business, and your output will be relatively easy to see.

Big corporations are the opposite of startups in almost every way. They are your best bet for a good work-life balance, and usually the salaries are pretty competitive. The day-to-day work is a lot more structured, and your position is more defined. Your job is also a lot safer, in terms of being laid off, and you are better protected. However, this also means that most of the time, you are a small cog in a huge machine. An important cog, yes, but it can still feel impersonal and transactional.

Medium-sized companies, meaning anywhere between 50 and 1,000 employees, tend to be a mix between the two. Where exactly this mix falls can only be determined on a case-by-case basis. Note that sometimes departments from large companies behave relatively independently, meaning you might find a perfect mix between the flexibility of a small company and the safety of a big corporation. You just have to explore the job market a bit.

In order to find one job, you need to apply to a lot of jobs. And I do mean *a lot*. Depending on where you are located and your experience, you should expect that around 100 applications will lead to around ten interviews, and that will lead to one job offer. So it is all a numbers game. Try not to take things personally, and do not be discouraged by rejection. Just think of it as bringing you one step closer to your actual job.

Recruiters will also contact you. Also known as head-hunters, they will try to reach you through LinkedIn, email, and phone calls. I am not saying that you should ignore them. But remember that companies prefer to hire you directly, if they can. First of all, never pay a recruiter. They are being paid by the companies, and their role is to sell you into a position. Since they are paid only if they get you hired, they have little interest as to whether you are a good fit for the company, or if the company is a good fit for you. So they do not have your best interests at heart.

The best piece of advice that I have for you here is to trust your instincts. They evolved over millions of years to keep you safe. So if somethings smells fishy or seems too good to be true, find out more. Head over to glassdoor.com, for example, and see what other employees have to say about that company. This will minimize the risks.

Interviews

Once you have started applying for jobs, it is a matter of time before you get your tech interview. Just because the interview is for a technical position does not mean that it will be radically different than any other interview. At the end of the day, an interview is about finding a good match. That includes technical skills of course, but it also includes compatibility with the company's culture, potential integration and smooth day-to-day interactions with the team, and so on.

The following sections explore what you can expect from such interviews, and tips for doing well. This includes what your general attitude should be, and what types of things you should also ask and be on the lookout for.

Most interviews include a coding challenge, which usually happens before the discussion happens. In this coding challenge, you are provided with a short list of requirements for a web app that you have to build. Your code should be easy to read and should use the proper libraries for your features (such as React). In addition, your solution must meet the requirements that were laid out.

I only accept challenges that I am relatively confident that I can finish in two-three hours. One challenge that I particularly enjoyed was to create a frontend application that loaded data from a given GraphQL endpoint, and was present it, with the possibility to filter the data, using a text input. That took me around an hour to do. I have also received challenges that would have taken me a couple of days, such as creating an entire mobile application, with highly-complex backend architectures, including deployment. I tend to reject those types of challenges.

I believe in the concept of equality. The hiring party wants you as an employee, just as much as you want to work there, as far as you know. They listed an opened position, and you applied for it. If you are ready to give four hours of your time to see if it's a good match, they should take the same time. I consider this a question of respect. I have no problem with an interview that lasts four hours, but to ask someone up-front for a 6- or 12-hour commitment, just to potentially be rejected using a generic email with no feedback, I find to be a big red flag.

One the other hand, sometimes there are 100 candidates for a single job, so you somehow need to filter through them. On my current team, we also have a similar challenge, but it can usually be achieved in fewer than an hour of work. My advice to you is to be careful about the time that you spend on such challenges and weigh whether they are worth it.

Once you jump through these hoops, it is time to meet the developers. Companies typically assign two-three developers from the team to assess your skills and compatibility. Every interview will start with a small introduction. When it is your time to talk, keep in mind that most likely they have seen your CV. Use three-four minutes to describe your CV, your achievements, and what motivates you. I, for example, mention the last few positions and companies that I worked for, and then generally describe how I love working in the tech industry because it enables other people to do their jobs better. I try to create products that people use, not just apps and code. I also have a more holistic approach to development in general. This is what I believe, and if we do not match on this level, it is better to find out earlier in the interviewing process.

Then next step is to present your answer to the challenge. Try to be mindful of everybody's time and start with a small demo. Include a two-three minute description of your code and explain how you pieced it together. After this point, the questions will start, first related to the challenge, then to wider technical topics, and then to general interviewing questions.

When you are asked a complex or technical question, first reiterate the problem, so that you can make sure that you understood everything completely. Then, while you think about possible solutions, talk about any ideas you have. Try to be as verbose as possible; the main reason for an interview is for the company to understand the way that you think. Go into detail and ask for clarification, if you see the need.

It is equally important for a potential employer to find out how you work on a team. Be open and relaxed. Most projects are team efforts, so you need to be able to work well on a team. Some of the most frequently asked questions are along the lines of "Can you tell me of a time that you had to work with a difficult person?" or "Can you tell me some of your achievements on your current team?". The interviewer is trying to find out how well you work as part of a greater organization, and how much they can rely on you to take care of tasks and issues without too much supervision.

I advise you to prepare at least one example of difficult situations or people from your professional experience, and an example of how you helped the team perform better. The latter usually involves you seeing a potential need in the way that the you and your colleagues work together, and finding a solution that ends up being implemented. Even writing documentation about processes falls into this category.

Another very common question employers might ask is why do you want to work for them. That is why it is important to do your homework. Look the company up before the interview, and if possible, even the product or department that you are interviewing for. Just take five minutes to go through the job posting again and prepare an answer for such a question. Because it will come up, in one form or another, more often than not.

Along similar lines, they might ask you why you are leaving your current position. This comes up so often, that I usually just incorporate it in my opening lines. It makes sense for a company to know what motivates you to switch jobs, so that they can also see some potentially red flags from their end, like people switching jobs very often.

On the subject of switching jobs too often, one rule of thumb is that it will take a new employee around six months to start being productive on a team. After that, they should at least bring in double the effort that was put into them. So that means that changing your job sooner than a year and a half will most likely be a red flag on your CV. If that is the case, I suggest you directly address this issue, before you're asked. It will make you look more trustworthy.

Ask questions. Especially at the end of the discussion, after they have asked all of their questions. An interview goes both ways, and it is important for you to see if you will fit into this new team. This also shows the interviewing party that you are interested in the job, attentive, and interactive. I always ask two questions at the end, and they are always the same ones:

1. What is your favorite part about working for company X?

2. What is your least favorite part about working for company X?

It is surprising how many times I have determined that I actually do not want to work for that company. Just by asking these questions, I found out issues related to pay, for example, or about common overtime, and so on. It is important that you go into a job knowing the ups and downs.

In addition, when you find some time, try searching for potential technical interview questions. Focus on JavaScript and SQL. The more interviews you have, the better you'll become at them. Take your time and trust the process. After each interview, try to figure out how you could have done better.

Summary

Getting a job is never easy. You have to filter through a lot of job positions, go though many interviews, negotiate, and generally keep trying. Not the most pleasant of activities, but it is mostly worth it.

This chapter looked into how to apply for a job and what to expect from an interview. I highly encourage you to do your own research as well and look up tips and tricks related to interviews.

CHAPTER 11

Working on a Team

The day will arrive when you start your first job as a web developer. This chapter discusses what exactly a web development team does differently than what you have been doing as an independent developer. This includes a discussion of how teams are set up and what the normal workflow is. The chapter also includes a short introduction to the technologies needed for modern web development in the context of team work and collaboration. I do, however, treat project management as a separate topic altogether. It's covered in the next chapter.

Team Structure

The most common way of working at the moment, when it comes to software development, is by using the *Agile methodology*. You will read a larger explanation about it a bit later, but the gist of it is that a team should be able to work relatively independently. That is, they should be able to take a feature from the stage of concept, into development, testing, deployment, and monitoring, without depending on other teams.

Usually, a development team will include a variety of roles in order to function properly, but many of them can be fulfilled by a single person. I have personally worked on teams that were as large as 13 people, as well as on teams of only three people. Regardless of the size of the team, one way or another, all of the roles were covered by someone.

© Radu Nicoara 2023
R. Nicoara, *How to be a Web Developer*, https://doi.org/10.1007/978-1-4842-9663-9_11

Consider what a typical development team looks like, in terms of roles that need to be fulfilled:

- *Software engineers* (one-eight positions per team). These people actually do the work of taking the different tasks from the team and build the features or the application that the team is assigned to. Most of what is covered in this book applies to this role. It sometimes can be further split into a frontend and a backend role, especially in large companies, but most small and middle-sized companies prefer to hire fullstack developers.

- *The network/infrastructure engineer* (one position). Once the application code is written, it somehow needs to be brought live, so that the users can access it. This is usually the job of the infrastructure engineer. They are the ones who make the initial setup of any project, implement monitoring, verify that the security of the application is in order, and set up the deployment pipeline.

- *The lead developer/architect* (one position). This role can also be filled by one of the developers and does not necessarily need to have managerial attributes attached to it. This person has a lot of experience and keeps an eye out for how all the pieces of the software puzzle fit together. They are also the ones with an overview of the entire application, which also means that they are the first contact point when it comes to technical topics related to the application.

- *The project manager/business analyst* (one position). This person represents the business needs of the company. They plan the two week sprints, open and prioritize the tickets, and so on. The next chapter is dedicated entirely to this job.

In addition to these positions, which one way or another will have to be completed by someone, there are also other positions that might or might not appear, but that are common in the industry.

- *The tester* (one-two positions). This person takes care of writing automated tests, and sometimes executes the manual tests, if needed. Since they are responsible for the proper running of the application, sometimes monitoring falls into their court as well.

- *The Agile coach* (one position). Usually a person who has the sole job of organizing the sprints and daily standups. The person's work is usually split between multiple teams.

- *The designer or UX/UI* (one position). The necessity of having a person who takes care of the user side of things is easy to understand. This person is usually found either on teams that build software with a large amount of users, or software that is relatively complicated.

But as mentioned, most of these positions can be filled by a single person. This is especially true when there are budget constraints, or when the roles don't require somebody separate just for that specific role.

The Lifecycle of a Feature

Before you start working on a feature, you first need to know what that feature is supposed to look like, and what it is supposed to do. This section quicky explores what exactly the process is, through which you arrive at a new feature being deployed.

The first step is often the request for a feature. Whether it was requested directly by a user, or by a member of your team, it will be saved into a *user story*. This is a type of ticket where you detail exactly the way the new feature will impact the user's activity. Whether you are talking about the ability to write comments, reply to conversations, or an easier way to find a button, you have to detail the task from the user's perspective.

Once that is done, if the case requires it, you should look at the *user interface* side. That means, ideally, making sure that there is a Figma design or a wireframe detailing the layout and the basic interaction flow of your new feature.

After this part is done, it is time for a *technical scoping*. This means that a developer will be assigned to create a document detailing the plan for the implementation. This generally means investigating any technologies that might be needed to implement the new features, in addition to any other issues. It is also useful at this step to develop a general GraphQL schema proposal, detailing the way that the backend and frontend will interact. Any uncertainties coming from the user or business side of things should also be resolved. After all this is written down, the technical scoping is then presented to the other developers, and the team must agree on a way of moving froward. It might sound like a lot of work, but this step is not needed every time. It's necessary only with very complex and large requests.

Once these issues have been cleared up from the business side of things, it is now time to develop. I recommend starting with the backend when developing, as it's usually the most complex. After that is done, you can then continue with the *frontend* side of your request. That is, bringing the backend changes to the users. After that is also done, it is time for you to write *unit tests*, and then manually perform the *user acceptance tests* on your end. Be sure to go through the user story and make sure that the points have been properly implemented. The last development step is to write any end-to-end tests that you need.

How You Develop

Normally, every application will have a certain set of live copies. This is just to keep things clean and to protect the production environment.

- *Local environment.* This will run on your personal machine and will try to approximate the development environment as much as possible. But in this case, since it is on your computer, you are the one in charge. You can modify the services and data, change the code, and generally do with the whole system as you please.

- *Development environment.* This runs on the cloud, and you can play around with it. Once the changes that you made are ready to be deployed, they will usually be delivered here. You will also be running a series of tests on dev, to make sure that everything works as intended. It usually contains either mock data or old data that is being synced once every few weeks or months.

- *Validation environment* (optional). This is usually a cleaner version of dev, where new features can be tested with the users. The validation environment is treated as a production environment that you can tweak if necessary. It is also used as a rehearsal for deploying to production.

- *Production environment.* The actual app that your users connect to. It contains the live data, the live APIs, and the frontend. It is also treated as a single point of truth.

When developing your code, most likely you will have a locally running environment with a frontend, backend, and a local database. This should simulate your development environment relatively well. In this local environment, you will develop your new features, test them, and then prepare to launch them into development.

So, how does your code go from your local computer to the production environment? As you are developing, your colleagues will be developing things in parallel. So you can't just push your new code on the server and declare it to be the new version of your application. Anybody who had developed something based on the previous version would lose their work.

For this purpose, you use a versioning tool, which provides all of the functionalities needed by the entire team. The most common versioning tool is Git. It allows multiple people to work on the same file at the same time and includes tools for merging the changes and resolving conflicts. It basically creates a copy of the codebase on your computer, and then registers the difference between the base branch and the one that you are working on.

Before you start working, you usually create a Git branch out of the current state of the code in dev. The name of the branch should be something representative and should start with your initials:

```
git checkout -b rn_new_comment_feature
```

You create and test your code on the local environment, just as you did before, and then commit your changes. You push the changes to the origin, meaning back to the original Git server:

```
git add * // adding all files to the branch
git commit -a -m "My Commit Message Here"
git push origin
```

The last command returns an URL that enables you to create a merge request (see Figure 11-1).

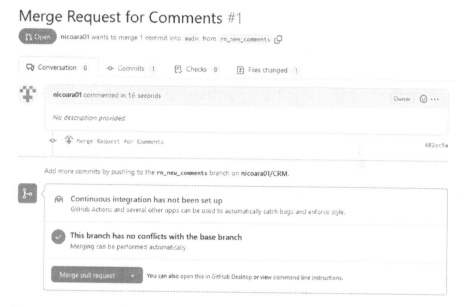

Figure 11-1. A merge request in GitHub

Once the merge request is done, you should always perform a self-review first, to make sure that you did not push anything by accident that you did not intend to push.

Go to the Files Changed tab (see Figure 11-2) and view the changes that the current merge request is trying to push into the codebase. Read the changes and perform a sanity check on your end.

Figure 11-2. *The Files Changed tab in the merge request*

Once you have ensured that everything is in order, you ask one of your colleagues to review the code as well. It is generally required, and a good idea, that at least two people (sometimes even more) review a piece of code before it reaches the main branch.

What exactly are you looking for, when you are reviewing a merge request? There are multiple levels on which you assess a merge request. These are, in no particular order:

- **Design**: Is the code well designed and appropriate for the system that it is being delivered to?

- **Functionality**: Does the code behave as the developer intended? Are there any unforeseen consequences of the way that the code is written, such as bugs or vulnerabilities?

- **Complexity**: Would another developer understand what the code is doing without further explanation?

- **Tests**: Does the code need any additional tests? Or should any of the current tests be modified?

- **Naming**: Did the developer choose clear names for classes, methods, variables, and so on?

- **Documentation**: Were the relevant documents updated? Is there any need for further clarification about the code?

Once these points have been reviewed, the appropriate person will approve the merge request. From this point, you can simply merge your branch into the main branch. Just click the green Merge button and Git will take care of the rest.

If the repository is set up in such a way, merging will also trigger certain additional steps. These are usually automated steps required to bring the new code live to the development environment.

The collection of steps that Git runs after a successful merge is called a *pipeline* (see Figure 11-3).

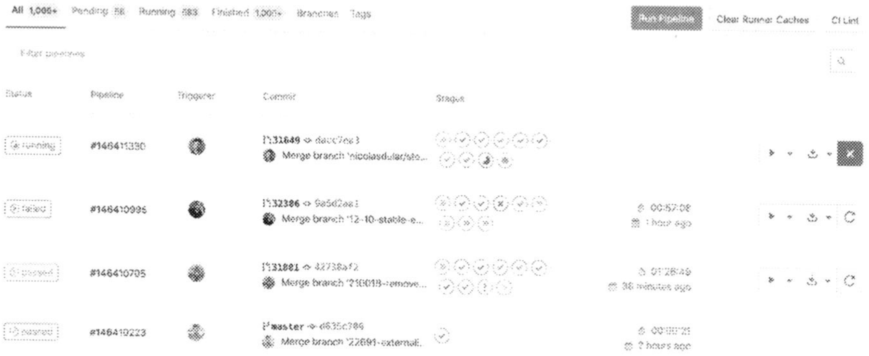

Figure 11-3. *Example provided by GitLab of some pipelines that are being run after a merge*

Here are some additional pieces of advice that I have for someone starting their development career and working on a technical team:

- **Communicate when something looks like a bad idea.** The entire team relies on you and your experience to raise awareness about any roadblock that might appear in the future.

- **Try to get involved with the cycles of an application.** Try learning more about UX, about infrastructure, and whatever else you are in contact with. Be curious!

- **Avoid technical terms as much as possible.** The main purpose of communicating is to relay information. Therefore, make sure that there are as few blocks as possible, and simplify your speech as much as you can, especially with people who are not well versed in your field.

- **Do not be too attached to your ideas.** Ask the team for a vote if there is no way to achieve a consensus, and once the vote is done, go with the decision. Even if you do not agree with it. That is what makes someone a great team-player.

Another concept that is currently gaining a lot of traction is *pair programming*. This mean that a certain feature is being built by two developers at the same time, on the same computer. Usually, one is the *driver*, meaning that they are the ones writing the code, and the other one is the *navigator*, meaning they dictate the way the logic of the code should run. The advantage of using pair programming is that testing and reviewing are usually done very quickly, as each piece of code has been seen by at least two sets of eyes. This also makes the code more robust and minimizes potential bugs. The disadvantage, of course, is that the team can now only deliver half of their theoretical speed, so it is absolutely a matter of quality vs quantity. If a team has pair programming as a standard, or it is only happening with major algorithmic difficulties.

Summary

Working on a team is generally a challenge for a lot of people. But it is one of the most important parts of almost any job. Your superpower as a human relies on how well you can collaborate with others.

Hopefully, this chapter provided you with some insights into how web developers work on a team to achieve their goals, and what you can do to help once you are hired.

CHAPTER 12

Project Management Methods

They say that a team is only as good as the one who leads it. I would say that a team is only as good as the way it's organized. Knowing what you will work on today and the way that relates to the rest of the team can make the difference between a mediocre team and a great one. This chapter explores how modern project management works in organizing IT development.

The Agile Methodology

The Agile methodology is the current industry standard in terms of web development. That is because it can deliver results significantly faster than the old way of working. Before you start learning about the new way of working, it's a good idea to review the old ways.

Twenty years ago, new software applications were completed and then handed over the date of the launch. By then, the entire project was done. Developers had already planned the entire thing, written the code, tested the app, debugged it, and implemented any fixes. It took a significant amount of time just to have everything planned out, planning which itself sometimes would take a couple of months.

With Agile, developers integrate pieces of code a little at a time. The process has moved from this cumbersome, monolith approach, to building regular, small iterations into the software development process. This

© Radu Nicoara 2023
R. Nicoara, *How to be a Web Developer*, https://doi.org/10.1007/978-1-4842-9663-9_12

approach is usually called *Agile*. This is in contrast to the large and linear approach of project management used 20 years ago, called *waterfall*. This can be summarized as a linear approach to development, where everything is preplanned, and each new step required the previous step to be finished.

Agile software development is an umbrella term that encompasses any set of processes and procedures that follow the 12 rules of Agile, as they are derived from the Agile Manifesto [3]. Those rules are as follows:

1. "Our highest priority is to satisfy the customer through early and continuous delivery of valuable software.

2. Welcome changing requirements, even late in development. Agile processes harness change for the customer's competitive advantage.

3. Deliver working software frequently, from a couple of weeks to a couple of months, with a preference to the shorter timescale.

4. Business people and developers must work together daily throughout the project.

5. Build projects around motivated individuals. Give them the environment and support they need, and trust them to get the job done.

6. The most efficient and effective method of conveying information to and within a development team is face-to-face conversation.

7. Working software is the primary measure of progress.

8. Agile processes promote sustainable development.
    The sponsors, developers, and users should be able
    to maintain a constant pace indefinitely.

9. Continuous attention to technical excellence and
    good design enhances agility.

10. Simplicity—the art of maximizing the amount of
    work not done—is essential.

11. The best architectures, requirements, and designs
    emerge from self-organizing teams.

12. At regular intervals, the team reflects on how to
    become more effective, then tunes and adjusts its
    behavior accordingly."

As an example that perfectly encompasses the spirit of Agile
development, consider the following scenario.

Imagine that your task is to build an airplane. You might be persuaded
to start working on the landing gear first, then on the wings, the cockpit,
and so on. At the end, you would put everything together and start testing.
You run a few tests and fix everything there is to fix. After a long period of
waiting, the customer can finally try out the product.

This approach, however functional, means that you have a functioning
product only at the end, and that the customer has nothing to work on, and
nothing to give feedback on in the meantime.

A better approach is to build some rudimentary wings first, put a
harness on them, and build a hang glider. You would then hand this over to
the user for testing and gather feedback. Then, as you start working on the
fuselage, you attach the previously built wings to it and build a glider. After
this point, as you start working on an engine, you attach the fuselage to the
aircraft and have a small propeller plane. And at the end of it all, as you
scale up, you can create an airliner or a jumbo jet.

As you can see in Figure 12-1, from the very start, the customer has a flying device. Although it may not be able to do everything, it is useful and you can gather feedback as you improve the product. It also allows you to incorporate any feedback into the newer versions of the product and frequently revise it.

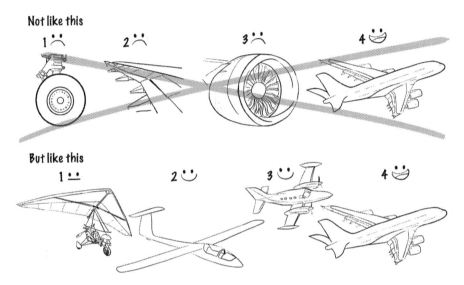

Figure 12-1. *Example of correct development [4]*

This is exactly the same process when it comes to software development. While development is happening, the customer can still use the product, even if it's not in its final form. If you were to approach development in the waterfall way, where you focus directly on the final product, that would mean that the first time you would receive feedback on the product, and the first time that the customer would use the product, would be at the end of the lifecycle. This stands fundamentally against the concept of Agile development, as it may lead to high rejection rates, and the product may not be what the customer needs.

There is no fixed process for Agile, and each team will have its own Agile Development method and its own ways of doing things. At least that much needs to be said. But with that in mind, this section explores the most common approaches and the concepts behind them.

At the core of the Agile methodology is the idea of continuous integration and continuous delivery (CI/CD). That means that every two to four weeks—a period that is called a *Sprint*—the team will have target features to add the main app, including the testing that such features require, integration, documentation, and so on.

These new consumable features should, first of all, not break any functionality that is already there. The team should also try to avoid launching incomplete features that error out when they are used.

Fundamentally, the target of the Sprint is the completion and deployment of separate components into the main application. This enables you to split an app into multiple incremental steps, so that you can easily adapt to any incoming changes or difficulties. This is what makes it agile.

Such an approach also allows you to integrate feedback very quickly.

At the end of every Sprint, the team goes through a ceremony (a meeting) called *Sprint planning,* where the project manager, together with the team, plans what the next Sprint should tackle, which tickets should be worked on, and what the goal of the next two weeks should be. It is also worth mentioning that the length of a Sprint usually is two weeks. A two-week Sprint brings a good balance between taking time for planning and having enough time for execution.

Each ticket should have a rough estimate of how many hours it will take to finish, including development, testing, bug fixing, and deployment. This estimate is approved by the team in a previous a meeting, called *grooming* or *backlog grooming* (or a variation of these). This is usually done one day before the planning. Each ticket is presented to the team, and everyone gets to vote on how much effort each of the tickets will require. If the ticket is open-ended, such as an improvement of a certain piece of code, the team will usually time-box the ticket.

Each day, early at the beginning of the workday, the team meets for what is called the *daily standup*. Every member takes turns explaining the state of their tickets, what they did the day before, and what their plan for the current day is. This provides transparency and good team cohesion. Each team member is also responsible for asking for help if they need it. See Figure 12-2.

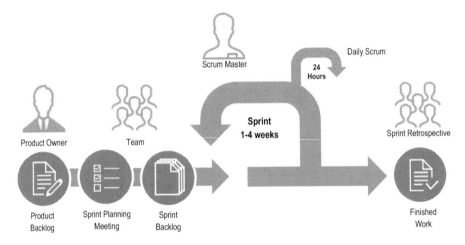

Figure 12-2. *The lifecycle of Scrum methodology*

Each time anybody finds a bug in the application, or something that needs to be improved in the code, they open a ticket, which goes in the *backlog*. It is then up to the project manager to prioritize the backlog, a process that is usually completed with the lead developer.

The *Sprint retrospective*, or simply the *retro,* is completed at the end of the Sprint. The team discusses the good and bad aspects of the previous Sprint and decides on how to improve the workflow.

The discussion is split into three distinct chapters. The first chapter is about what went well, where team members take note of the good things that happened, or the positive processes that should be continued. The next chapter is about what went bad, and this is usually where most of the discussion happens. The discussion is focused in such a way to determine what can be improved. Working in an Agile way also means that, for every issue the team is facing, there usually is a possible solution. Even if it is not perfect, the team can try one solution for two weeks, and at the next retro discuss whether it helped.

Here is an example of a retro board:

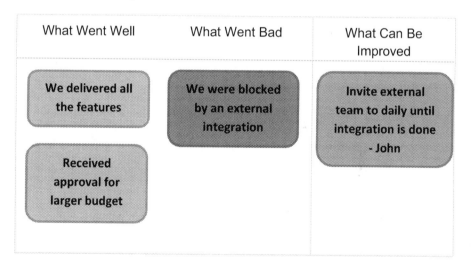

What Went Well	What Went Bad	What Can Be Improved
We delivered all the features	We were blocked by an external integration	Invite external team to daily until integration is done - John
Received approval for larger budget		

Usually, each column is opened up for editing one at a time, and each member of the team adds their items privately. Each item is then discussed with the entire team. The last column should also have someone assigned to handle it, so that someone is responsible for taking care of the task. Then, during the next retro, the previous decisions are reviewed and adjusted, if needed.

Summary

The Agile methodology in general, and Scrum in particular, are currently the industry standard in terms of web development. This involves Sprints that usually last two weeks, daily meetings to organize the team and bring everyone up to date, and features delivered regularly into the main working project. Compared to the old approach called waterfall, the Agile methodology allows you to incorporate feedback much earlier and be more flexible in terms of where the product is going.

PART IV

In Summary

CHAPTER 13

Conclusions

Now that our time together has come to an end, it's time to review the topics covered in our journey together. I started with a series of introductions into the career of a web developer, and you learned what you can expect when working in such an environment. You learned about the benefits and drawbacks of working as a programmer in general, together with some common misconceptions.

Next, you learned about the importance that a database holds for any given application, and how the SQL language generally works. You saw how a SELECT statement is created, what you can do in a WHERE clause, and probably one of the most important points of all—how to write a JOIN statement.

You then learned about GraphQL, which is a query language for APIs. You also learned about JavaScript, in order to understand how exactly this language operates, what makes it different, and what you can expect when using this language.

You then created your first backend application, using Node.js and GraphQL, and managed to get it connected to a database. You succeeded in setting up an entire environment, creating your first query, and then your first mutation.

Once you were done with the backend, you moved to creating your first frontend app. You used React to create a basic, bare-bones website, and then started adding different components to it, in order to give your fictious users an intuitive way to interact with the backend.

© Radu Nicoara 2023
R. Nicoara, *How to be a Web Developer*, https://doi.org/10.1007/978-1-4842-9663-9_13

After everything was done, you learned a bit about the world of testing, and learned what you can do to test your code. You learned about unit tests as well end-to-end tests.

That was the big chunk of theory in this book. With that out of the way, you investigated other technologies that you might need, if you will be engaging with the world of web development, and had a short introduction to where and how these technologies can be used.

Afterward, you learned how to prepare for your first job, what a normal interview looks like, how to write a CV that is attuned to web development positions, and how to find and apply to a job.

I also discussed your first day on the job. You learned how a development team works, how it is organized, and how a day-to-day work pace flows.

At the end, to wrap everything up, you learned about project management inside the field of software development, about Agile and Scrum, and about the way that a development team organizes itself in order for the team's goals to be met, and most importantly, the clients to be happy.

I wrote this book with the hope that I could expose you to the wonderful world of web development and that I could spark the same curiosity and interests that I myself felt, once I started to understand more about development in general.

This book should not be seen as a manual on how to use any particular programming language or framework, as this is not what I intended it to be. Instead, I wrote it as a guide for how and where to find more information once you start on the development path, and what your steps into the programming world should be. Since I had a difficult time figuring out what was important and what was not worth putting my time into, I hope that I have lightened the load for you, and that I at least gave you a rough map of the web development field.

But there is only one way to become good at anything in general, and programming is no exception to that rule. The only way to succeed is to keep on doing it, to try to expose yourself as much as possible, watch YouTube channels related to programming, and most important, start your own projects. Or at least to work on something that brings you joy, so that you can easily get motivated.

If you want to have a career in web development, or in any domain, the best advice I have for you is to keep on going and never give up. Even one small step every day will compound over the years and bring you places that you never thought were possible. So just take that small step each and every day.

As a final word, I want to thank you for the time that you set aside for our journey together, through the world of web development. I hope that this book provided some insights into what exactly web development is, and what you should expect if you want to join this lucrative career.

As I started in this domain without any type of formal education, I am certain that, as long as you enjoy building applications, web development can be a career that you will not only find worth perusing, but that will also bring you satisfaction.

References

[1] – https://www.statista.com/statistics/1124699/worldwide-developer-survey-most-used-frameworks-web/

[2] – https://blog.back4app.com/backend-programming-languages-list/

[3] – https://www.agilealliance.org/agile101/12-principles-behind-the-agile-manifesto/

[4] – Image created by Ruxandra Corduneanu

Index

Printed in the United States
by Baker & Taylor Publisher Services